The

Marriage Improvement Project

MIP

The

Marriage Improvement Project

GHP

GHP

The Marriage Improvement Project

This title is also available as a free download from the author's website - http://thepfjournal.wordpress.com

Requests for information should be addressed to:
Carey Green, P.O. Box 242, Leadville, Colorado, 80461

Cover Design: *Craig Pritchett*

Printed in the United States of America

Contents

To my Savior, Jesus – You have loved me in such an amazing, self-sacrificing way. Your example has taught me, again and again, how I am to love my dear wife... and it has served me so well. Thank You Lord, for such grace.

To my dear wife and partner, Mindi. You have been such a wise and powerful tool in the hand of our God. He has used you countless times to bring improvement to our marriage, and to bring me great joy in doing so. Thank you for your humble, wise, unchanging love and for always believing in me more than I do myself.

To my two lovely daughters, Melinda & Madeline, who helped me proof the text of this book. You are treasures to me...

How to Use This Book

This is a different kind of book...

This is a book for couples. It's written *to* couples, and *for* couples to read and complete together. If you are planning to read this book "solo" as one half of a marriage relationship, you will still benefit, but don't expect to get as much out of it as you would if you were going through it *with* your spouse.

Said another way... you are strongly encouraged to strongly encourage your spouse to complete this marriage improvement project *with* you. You marriage will benefit the most, if you do it together.

What this book is about

One of the most dominant images God uses in the scriptures to describe both His love for us and the type of relationship He desires to have with us, is the picture of marriage. Take a look...

> *For your Maker is your husband, the LORD of hosts is his name; and the Holy One of Israel is your Redeemer, the God of the whole earth he is called.*
> ***Isaiah 54:5***

> *Surely, as a treacherous wife leaves her husband, so have you been treacherous to me, O house of Israel, declares the LORD.*
> ***Jeremiah 3:20***

> *Husbands, love your wives, as Christ loved the church and gave himself up for her...*
> ***Ephesians 5:25***

Let us rejoice and exult and give him the glory, for the marriage of the Lamb has come, and his Bride has made herself ready;
Revelation 19:7

And I saw the holy city, new Jerusalem, coming down out of heaven from God, prepared as a bride adorned for her husband.
Revelation 21:2

When God peppers His word with the imagery of marriage like this, we have to consider the significance of what He's doing. He's using something familiar to us to teach us about something that is not as familiar to us. Marriage is the most intimate human relationship, and God intentionally chooses it to portray the type of relationship He desires to have with His people.

Our marriages are intended, by God, to be *representations* of His great love for His own people. The way a husband loves his wife and the way a wife responds to his love are meant to show others something of God's love for His people. That realization is thrilling and sobering at the same time.

It's thrilling when you realize that as married couples we have the great *privilege* of showing others the love of God. Imagine it in your day to day life: when your children, your friends, and your neighbors see you – a married couple – interacting with each other, they have the opportunity to see a picture of the unbelievable love of God, fleshed out in a human relationship right before their eyes! What a wonderful opportunity we have as married couples!

It's sobering when you realize that as married couples we have the great *responsibility* of showing others the love of God. It's our duty... our job... and we need to do it well.

In the pages to come, you'll find teaching and exercises attached to a variety of subjects. It is my greatest hope that these studies and the conversations that flow from them will enable the two of you to better love one another, and in so doing better represent God's great love for His people.

But the work you do will not only be for the sake of others. What you learn and apply will also benefit of your own marriage. Be a student of these issues for your own joy and happiness. It is exactly that kind of joy that will best represent God's devotion to His bride.

As you begin, know this: The Lord of all creation is present to teach you, guide you, and help you. It's His power that will enable you to do what you need to in order to grow your marriage. He's more than able to right any wrongs and clean up any mess – and He won't even break a sweat doing it! With Him, all things are possible (*Matthew 19:26*). Move ahead *trusting Him* to do what only He can do.

Make it a project

Have you ever had an important project of some type that you absolutely had to get done? It may have been an assignment at work, a ministry endeavor at church, or a home improvement project. Those kinds of projects require a relatively brief, but focused time of intensity for the sake of getting the job done.

You make it a top priority, grit your teeth (at times), and muscle through until it is done. It requires drive, determination, and self-discipline. When the dust settles, and you look on what you've accomplished, you experience the satisfaction of knowing that you've done something difficult and strenuous, but very significant.

It will be helpful if you think of this book as a "*marriage improvement project*" that you need to knuckle down and complete in the next 40 to 60 days. Don't misunderstand, it's not something you muscle through without having your heart in it. That won't do you any good, because marriage is a relationship meant to be lived from the heart.

This "*marriage improvement project*" is something you should do for your own sake, your spouse's sake, your marriage's sake, and for the Lord's greater glory. When your marriage becomes more of what God intended, both of you will be more joyous, content, and satisfied in the calling of marriage, and the Lord will be honored as a result.

You are going to be challenged to apply what **God thinks** to **your** marriage! The outcome of your obedience will be blessing, fruitfulness, and joy as you experience your marriage growing and maturing under the Lord's faithful care. You'll also faithfully demonstrate the wisdom of God in action, in the closest of human relationships.

How this book is organized

Husband and wife are to complete the daily assignments on their own, as their partner is doing the same. Then, on given days, you'll be instructed to discuss certain issues you've been studying, and how they relate to the specifics of your marriage. In this way you will both be learning the same things, and will be able to work together to implement those truths into your marriage.

Each day's work will include:

- A daily prayer suggestion (to help you point your mind and spirit in the right direction).
- Scripture passages relevant to the day's topic.
- Teaching about the passage.
- Illustrations and examples to help you bring the truth

you're learning into "real life."

- Questions for your prayerful consideration, discussion, and application.

As you prayerfully and honestly spend concentrated effort working on your marriage over the next 40 to 60 days, I pray you will find your God-empowered efforts to be the catalyst He uses to revive, restore, or revolutionize your relationship! Consider this study to be a marriage intensive, a prolonged counseling session designed to give your marriage a concentrated boost of life!

Helpful Tips

Before you dive in, here are some pointers on how to go about this study:

Set aside sufficient time. Each daily section will require 30 to 45 minutes.

Find a place that is quiet and free from distractions.

Make your daily time one of your top priorities.

Use a notebook to answer the questions thoughtfully & honestly.

Ask God to teach you as you begin each day's work.

Communicate with each other about your progress so you can stay on track together.

Finish the study! Don't quit! Trust the Lord to see you through!

Acknowledgments

Very few of the truths or principles in this study originate with me. Primarily, they come from the scriptures. I figure the Creator of marriage knows more about marriage than anyone else... so we'd be wise to seek His counsel on the matter! But that doesn't mean there aren't secondary sources He used in helping me put the MIP together.

To start off, I've gleaned a ton of insight from the things he's done in my life and marriage. My wife Mindi is one of the best teachers on marriage around... and I owe her a huge debt of gratitude for the many ways she's helped me understand marriage.

I also borrowed the foundational understanding behind the first 3 sections from Pastor Jimmy Evans' book, "*Marriage on the Rock*." You can find that book and a ton of other great resources for your marriage at he and his wife Karen's marriage ministry website: ***www.marriagetoday.org***.

The section on communication is heavily indebted to H. Norman Wright's book, "*Communication: Key to Your Marriage*." You can find that book and many other great books and curriculum at his website: ***www.hnormanwright.com***.

The sections toward the end that cover the roles of husband and wife in the marriage relationship are gleaned from a few different sources. First, is Pastor John Piper, whose teaching on 1 Peter 3 has greatly helped me know how to explain the biblical concept of submission in marriage.[1] In addition, I have found an incredible amount of helpful, scholarly biblical work in the writings of Dr. Wayne Grudem, in particular his book, "*Evangelical Feminism & Biblical Truth*."[2]

Last, but certainly not the least important, are the many couples that Mindi and I have been privileged to counsel and coach over the years. We have learned much about the Bible's approach and teaching on Christian marriage through laboring with these couples through the circumstances and issues in their lives. Thanks to all those couples who have allowed us into their lives, for the sake of our King's glory being seen in their marriages.

As you begin, I pray the Lord's richest blessing upon you, as you endeavor to grow in your love for each other, and in your representation of His love for His people!

Carey Green

1 http://www.desiringgod.org/resource-library/sermons/the-beautiful-faith-of-fearless-submission

2 http://store.ps.edu/products/Evangelical-Feminism-%26-Biblical-Truth-by-Dr.-Wayne-Grudem.html

1

SECTION ONE

Marriage First

DAY 1

A Prayer Suggestion: Begin today's study by thanking God for the opportunity to learn more of His heart about marriage. Ask Him to lead you as you consider the reading today!

Genesis 2:24

Therefore a man shall leave his father and his mother and hold fast to his wife, and they shall become one flesh.

Priorities. Every one of us has any number of greater and lesser priorities in our lives. Marriage is one of those priorities. But where does it fall on the scale of importance? Should it be toward the top, or the bottom, or somewhere in the middle? Today we are going to consider the place of priority that God intends your marriage to hold in your life.

Marriage came into being as one of the first acts of God's plan for all of history. After creating the world and the animals, God created the first man, Adam. But, Adam was alone, and God said that was not a good thing (*Genesis 2:18*).

To solve the problem, God created the first woman, Eve, and the first marriage was the result. In establishing marriage God created the first and most intimate human relationship, one which takes highest priority among all human relationships.

That idea is what we'll be referring to as "*The Marriage First Principle.*"

The Marriage First Principle

Genesis 2:24

Therefore a man shall leave his father and his mother and hold fast to his wife

There are 4 points to be made regarding *the Marriage First Principle*. We will be focusing on the first one today...

1. Your marriage relationship comes before all other earthly relationships.

Did you notice that our verse *instructs* a man to leave his father and mother when he gets married? It may sound like a silly command, since most people naturally do leave their parents when they marry. But it's important to realize that God says what He says, in the way that He says it, for a reason. There is no such thing as a "minor" idea in the scriptures. So when God tells a man to leave his father and mother when he marries, He's doing so for a reason.

What is He telling us by saying it this way? Does it mean that once a man gets married he is not allowed to live with or near his parents? It was very normal in the Old Testament for extended families to live together in the same camp, so that can't be what God meant. So what *does* it mean?

Consider this: The relationships that a person has with their mother and father are normally the closest relationships they've had prior to adulthood. In teaching us that a man is to "leave" his father and mother, God is saying that once a couple becomes married, they are moving into a new and different stage in life, where the close relationships of the past (with parents) are to take a lesser place of importance in view of the new relationship that has begun (marriage).

There are many applications of this that we will address in the days to come, but for today it is important to understand that this is the basic idea behind *the Marriage First Principle*. Let's flesh the idea out a bit.

You have many relationships that fill your life – relationships with extended family members, co-workers, neighbors, friends, children – and every one of them is important in it's own way, and to varying degrees. But what *the Marriage First Principle* teaches us is that as important as those relationships may be, *none* of them is to rival your relationship with your spouse. Your spouse is to come first...in your thoughts and in your consideration. In the days ahead you'll learn more about how this looks in everyday life.

Questions for Reflection

- Restate *the Marriage First* principle in your own words.

- Do you believe that God is calling YOU to make your marriage the TOP human relationship in your life?

- Are you willing to take the time to learn what it will take for your marriage to be that kind of priority?

- Make a quick list of the major relationships in your life. After you've compiled your list, rank them in two ways. First, rank them in order of how important they are to you currently. Second, rank them in order of how you think God desires them to be.

- Where was your marriage relationship on the first ranking? Where is it on the second ranking?

- Stop right now and ask God to give you a heart to understand and embrace what **<u>He</u>** has in mind for you in this area.

DAY 2

A Prayer Suggestion: Ask the Lord to prepare you for the lessons He has for you today... even though they may be difficult to swallow!

In the last lesson we were introduced *the Marriage First Principle* as revealed to us in Genesis 2:24. Let's look at the passage again...

Genesis 2:24

Therefore a man shall leave his father and his mother and hold fast to his wife, and they shall become one flesh.

The idea behind *the Marriage First Principle*, very simply put, is this...

1. The marriage relationship comes before all other relationships.

Consider that truth again, in light of the many relationships you have. Children, parents, close friends, co-workers, neighbors. In order for your marriage relationship to be over and above all of those in terms of importance, there is likely a good deal of change that needs to happen – in the way you think about marriage, and the way you act as a result.

Today we are going to spend the majority of our time, doing something very simple, but not necessarily easy. Today we will be applying this principle to the real circumstances of your life. That brings us to the second point to be made regarding *the Marriage First Principle*:

2. The *Marriage First p*rinciple must be carried out *practically*, not just in words.

I don't have to tell you that life is busy. In a given week, your schedule is likely very, *very* full. What I'd like to ask you is this: Can you admit to yourself that you can't do it all? There is only so much of you to go around, and only so much time. The demands of life are beyond your ability to meet on your own.

In light of that, all of us have to make some hard choices in regard to our time and energy in order to make sure that what *is* truly important is what is *being done* in our lives. There is no way around it...some of the lesser things in life have to go, so that the more important, vital things in life can stay. Those are hard choices to make. They are *sacrifices* that have to be made.

Your marriage relationship is to be the highest value relationship you have. Your parents or siblings, who were likely among the closest relationships you had before getting married, are still very important – but not as important as your spouse.

Though it seldom happens this way, if you ever have to make a choice between your parents and your spouse, or your siblings and your spouse – your spouse wins, hands down! It's not because you don't love your parents or siblings, but because you love your spouse more. That's the way God intends it to be when you marry... you leave father and mother and cleave to your spouse. A new priority relationship is born!

Naturally, it takes a good deal of adjustment for *the Marriage First Principle* to become a reality. Not only will each of you have to adjust in order for your marriage to come first...your extended family will have to adjust too! It's entirely possible, and quite common, that they'll have a hard time adjusting to your new priority. But you can lead them to understand by your example and through the conversations you have. As they see and hear your commitment to your marriage's importance, they'll begin to get it themselves.

All of that is the relational side of *the Marriage First Principle* that was covered in the last lesson. But today you need to realize that your marriage relationship should not only come before other relationships, it should also come before other *things*. Said another way, no person ***or*** thing should ever take a higher place of importance than your marriage relationship.

If your marriage relationship is to be that kind of priority, you'll have to show it to be so in practical ways, not just in words. That means that some hard choices need to be made in order to ensure that your marriage relationship is receiving the time and attention that it needs as your top priority. In most cases, that will require sacrifice on a variety of levels.

Think of it this way: In light of your marriage relationship being first, your spouse could very appropriately ask you, "What will you give up in order to make me first?" And you could ask the same of them. That's another way of saying to each other, "My relationship with you comes before everything else."

But be careful that you don't misunderstand. It's not that your other responsibilities or obligations are not important. Many of them are extremely important in God's eyes (take your children, or your work for examples). The point is that as important as those things may be, they are not *as* important as your relationship with your spouse.

Your spouse will naturally, and *rightly* resent anything that takes their God-given place at the top of your priority list. Nothing else should ever be allowed to crowd them out of that place.

Think of the practical implications... Work, time, hobbies, recreation – all of them have to take a back-seat to your marriage relationship. That doesn't mean that you never do those kinds of things, but that you take care of your marriage *first*.

For example: If a special retreat or activity is planned for one spouse, and the other spouse has a personal need arise at the same time, the activity has to go so that the needs of the spouse can be first. If work schedules are such that you never get time together as a couple, then something about the work schedules needs to change so that you can. These are examples of what it means to carry out your commitment to your marriage practically.

Questions for Reflection

There are all kinds of things that can crowd out essential time you need with your spouse to talk, plan, pray, care for one another, play, and simply be together. Reflect on your own situation as you *honestly* consider these questions...

- On a scale of 1 to 10 (1 = terrible, 10 = wonderful) how well are you doing at setting aside time to focus on your spouse/marriage in an average week?

- What kind of things need to happen in your personal schedule in order to ensure that your answer to the previous question improves?

Assignment

Set aside sufficient time to discuss the following questions with your spouse. Don't allow yourself to become defensive. This assignment is aimed at helping you work together as partners to improve your marriage relationship.

- On the same 1 to 10 scale, ask your spouse how well you are doing at setting aside time in an average week to focus on your relationship with them. Compare their answer to yours from the previous section. Discuss the reasons behind the differences in your answers.

- WORK ISSUES – in order for each of you to practically do what is needed in order for your marriage relationship to be first...
  - How many hours a day should each of you work?
  - What about extra hours or overtime? How much is too much?

- Are there any adjustments to your work schedules that can be made to create windows of time you can spend together for strengthening your marriage? Make sure you both give input.

- EVENING HOURS / WEEKENDS
  - Are you cramming your "off" time so full of activity and obligation that you are neglecting time together?
  - Is the T.V., computer, movies or some other form of entertainment/hobby consuming time that could be better spent in communication together or encouragement of each other?
  - Talk together about adjustments you can make that will enable you to be more available for time together.
  - If you need to, schedule your times together. Go ahead, write them down on your calendar like an appointment. It may feel artificial, but is very necessary if you are going to make your relationship the important thing it should be.
- COMMUNICATION
  - Have you established a daily pattern of communication so that you are both on the same page about your lives together?
  - Discuss ways/times you could do this daily so that you stay connected regarding the important issues of your lives together.

- CHILDREN
  - Do your children have a regular bed-time? If they don't you are likely robbing yourselves of some of the most valuable times you can have together at the end of the day. Discuss this together.

DAY 3

<u>*A Prayer Suggestion*</u>*:* Ask the Lord to give you conviction about the things you are learning, so that they are more than simply head knowledge!

We continue today, considering the implications of *the Marriage First Principle*, found in Genesis 2:24...

Genesis 2:24

Therefore a man shall leave his father and his mother and hold fast to his wife, and they shall become one flesh.

So far, we've seen two important points...

1. The marriage relationship comes before all other relationships.

2. The *Marriage First Principle* must be carried out *practically*, not just in words.

Today we will be considering another point that has to do with *the Marriage First Principle*... It has to do with things that might interfere with the rightful place of importance your marriage relationship should have. You may be surprised when you hear it...

3. Most of the things that lessen the priority of your marriage relationship are good things, not bad things.

It's easy to imagine Satan trying to disrupt the health and stability of your marriage relationship through some insidious or dark means that is blatantly evil in nature. But you need to realize that those kinds of attacks from our enemy, though they undoubtedly happen at times, are the exception rather than the rule. The things that most often distract us from maintaining a high priority on our marriages are the other good things that fill our lives. Let's consider a few...

Children – Children are a great blessing from the Lord, no doubt about that (*Psalm 127:3*). I have 5 kids – and am tremendously blessed with the unique and wonderful person each of them is! But whether young and still at home, or older and moved out on their own, children can easily become a higher priority than the ongoing health of the marriages which produced them!

Said practically, the needs of the kids can easily become the most time-consuming, dominant feature of your home, gobbling up the necessary time you need to ensure that your marriage relationship remains healthy. If your marriage is going to remain strong, you must learn the wise balance of being a good and faithful mom or dad, while still maintaining the vital connection as man and wife that God first began.

Consider these thoughts about your marriage as it relates to your children...

- Your Christ-centered marriage is the hub around which the wheel of your family revolves. If your marriage is not healthy, the family will fly apart!
- Your children are a temporary focus, but your marriage focus will endure your whole lifetime. You've probably known couples who didn't know how to relate to each other once their children had all left home. That's a

very sad condition for a Christian marriage, one I don't want you to experience!

- How can your children know what a good marriage relationship looks like if you don't demonstrate it to them? Sure, they need to know that they are loved by you, but there is a very healthy and godly security that they receive when they know that the two of you love each other first and foremost – and they will carry that understanding into their future marriage.

Don't misunderstand, time and attention that you give to your kids is important – but a healthy marriage will impact them with much greater power than anything else! Your healthy marriage serves as the fertile soil from which your children grow and mature. It provides them a stability and security that can only come in that way.

Work/Career – The last study and assignment addressed this issue to a degree, but there are some additional thoughts that may be helpful in re-thinking the priority your marriage needs to take over your work...

- Even your work is given to you for the sake of your family. It is the means by which God provides and cares for you and them. Don't let the "tool" (work) overwhelm the "project" (family) it is intended to help foster and maintain!
- Many people come home to refuel for another day at work... but in God's perspective, your real work begins when you walk through the door of your own house (Deuteronomy 6:4-9)! Take the time during the drive home to get your mind and spirit ready for the real job of home life. Don't let your work become a drain on what is truly important!

Church – Service in your local church is of vital importance to you and to your church family. I have been in full-time church ministry for almost my entire marriage, so I know that as well as anyone! *but*, your marriage comes first! I'd rather have a church full of healthy marriages than almost anything else – in part because a healthy church will flow out of those healthy families! Consider these possibilities when considering whether church activities may be overshadowing your marriage...

- If you go wrong here, your well-intentioned choices may cause others in the home to resent church activity, or worse, they may even come to resent God Himself!
- Marriage was God's first created institution (before the church).
- The church can only be built on healthy transformed families, which start with healthy marriages!

Questions for Reflection

- Write a list of the things (besides your marriage) that take up most of *your* time, thoughts, energy, emotional strength, etc.

- Evaluate your list. Is there anything on your list that is detracting from the "first place" nature of your marriage relationship? Be honest with yourself.

- Ask your spouse to evaluate your list according to the same criteria.

- Genuinely listen to your spouse as they explain their evaluation of your list. Avoid becoming defensive! Ask them, "How would *you* suggest I address this problem?" (This should include what needs to be removed or changed and what should be put in its place.)

- Humbly agree to do what they suggest. Consider it one of your first steps of "sacrifice" for the sake of the marriage.

DAY 4

<u>*A Prayer Suggestion*</u>*:* Begin by thanking the Lord for everything He has shown you so far regarding the importance of the priority of your marriage relationship. Ask Him to help you as you seek to apply His teaching...

Today we continue exploring the implications of *the Marriage First Principle* by looking at the 4th point of focus. But before we do, let's review our key passage and the previous 3 points...

Genesis 2:24

Therefore a man shall leave his father and his mother and hold fast to his wife, and they shall become one flesh.

1. The marriage relationship comes before all other relationships.

2. The *Marriage First Principle* must be carried out *practically*, not just in words.

3. Most of the things that lessen the priority of your marriage relationship are good things, not bad things.

The points we've looked at so far have had some very practical applications. Today's point will address the mindset behind those practical steps. It's about the conviction that fuels your commitment to keep your marriage relationship in its right priority. Here it is...

4. Both partners have a moral obligation to protect their relationship from all things and people that would threaten its "first place" position.

There will be many difficulties and obstacles in keeping your marriage a top priority. There will be many distractions that will pull at you to compromise the commitment to your marriage that you have begun to develop. If you are going to be successful in maintaining the priority of your marriage relationship you will have to do so out of a very deep sense of it being the *right* thing to do.

You must *know* without a doubt that it is God's intention for your marriage to thrive as you devote the time, energy, love, and thought to it that every healthy, strong relationship requires. He wants your marriage to thrive so that others can see His great love through it!

Some helpful thoughts...

- Intentionality is key! Nothing important in your life happens by accident. There is not a healthy relationship in the world that got that way without purpose and determination. Your marriage will be no different.
- Keeping your marriage at the top of the priority list will require diligence. Those days that you don't "feel" like putting in the effort, you must draw on the strength the Holy Spirit provides, and make the effort anyway! You'll be amazed what He does through that kind of obedient, dependent attitude!
- The dedication required to keep your marriage top priority will require time. There's no way around it. Continue making room in your schedule for each other so that your marriage can be what it is intended to be.

- At times, your commitment to a strong and healthy marriage will require self-sacrifice. Your own desires and wants will have to take a back seat to your marriage – and that is how it should be!
- Don't wait on your spouse to take the first steps in improvement. Before the Lord, you are responsible to do what is right – regardless of what your spouse does!
- In order to stay focused on your marriage you will have to periodically review your attitudes, schedule, lifestyle, and many other things to see if anything is out of adjustment. Do this regularly, together, so that both of you can understand the needs and heart of the other.
- Finally, and most importantly, you will need the Lord's help. Ask the Lord to help you day by day, as you endeavor to remain focused on doing your part to maintain a strong and healthy marriage. Said another way – don't take your marriage for granted. Make your marriage a daily prayer request!

Question for Reflection

- Have you become convinced in your mind and heart that your marriage must be one of your highest priorities?

- If so, what realizations have helped you to see it that way? If not, what do you think stands in the way?

Assignment

- Talk with your spouse about the previous two questions. Remember, be honest and open instead of defensive.
- Take the time to tell your spouse where you are in terms of your convictions about your marriage. It doesn't have to be eloquent or fancy... just real.

- Spend some time praying together, for your marriage. Ask the Lord to bring about His best in your relationship, for His glory!

DAY 5

<u>*A Prayer Suggestion*</u>*:* Ask the Lord to fill you with more of *His* desire to see your marriage to be all it can be!

This is our last day to focus on *the Marriage First Principle*, and we will use our time today to review and internalize what you've been learning and processing. To review...

Genesis 2:24
Therefore a man shall leave his father and his mother and hold fast to his wife, and they shall become one flesh.

1. The marriage relationship comes before all other relationships.

2. The *Marriage First Principle* must be carried out *practically*, not just in words.

3. Most of the things that lessen the priority of your marriage relationship are good things, not bad things.

4. Both partners have a moral obligation to protect their relationship from all things and people that would threaten its priority.

It is very important to begin this study with *the Marriage First Principle*. It helps to put first things first, because it clearly establishes one of the most foundational components to a healthy marriage and the reasons behind it. It is what enables you to remain steadfast – to keep your bearings through the difficulties you will face in your married life. It is what will help you to make wise choices that will benefit your marriage. It is what God says you are to do when you marry – to make your relationship with your spouse the most important human relationship you have.

In doing so, you pull back the curtain to reveal God's love for His people, so that the watching world can see and be drawn to Him!

Questions for Reflection

- How would you describe *the Marriage First Principle* in your own words?

- As you understand it, explain why this principle is so foundational.

- Which of the 4 main points stands out to you the most? Why do you think this is?

- When it comes to proving the priority of your marriage in practical ways, what have you discovered needs to change? Are you moving in that direction?

- Prayer with your spouse about this topic. Ask the Lord to help you both be and do what you need to be and do –for the sake of your marriage!

SECTION TWO

2

The Cleaving Principle

DAY 6

<u>A Prayer Suggestion</u>: Begin today by quietly sitting before the Lord. Let everything go. Trust Him to be your good Teacher today. Trust Him to lead you where you need to go in your time with Him.

Genesis 2:24

Therefore a man shall leave his father and his mother and hold fast to his wife, and they shall become one flesh.

Today we begin thinking about another truth for marriage that is implied in Genesis 2:24. The truth we covered in the last section focused on the phrase "*leave his father and mother.*" The phrase we are going to key in on this section is the phrase... "*hold fast to his wife*" - Genesis 2:24

The King James version words this a bit differently due to the type of language used when it was written. Instead of saying that a man is to "*hold fast*" to his wife, the KJV says a man is to "*cleave to his wife.*"

No, it has nothing to do with a meat cleaver... it's a much more important word than that. "*Cleave*" is not a word that is often used in our culture, so it's meaning may be a mystery to you. What does it mean to "*cleave*" to someone... for a man to "*cleave*" to his wife?

> **CLEAVE** – *to catch by pursuit: - follow close (hard after), be joined (together), keep (fast), overtake, pursue hard.*

The word clearly implies a chase or a pursuit - a seeking after. It reminds us of those long gone days of courtship.

Typically, it is the man who begins pursuing a young woman, showing off, trying to woo her, seeking to impress her. He does extra, special things for her (flowers, gifts, special notes or poems), and he might even give up some of his most treasured hobbies and things just to spend time with her or be near her. That is exactly the idea of the word "*cleave*."

Ladies, can you recall those days? What did it do to you to know that the guy you were interested in was seeking after you? It was flattering to know that he was interested in you, wasn't it? When your growing intimacy and the passing of time came together on the day that he finally proposed, your hopes were realized! He really did want you! In many ways, it was his consistency that paid off!

Sadly, that's about as long as it lasts, in many cases. It's not uncommon for men stop chasing their wives shortly after they are married. It is as if once they "have" them, the excitement of the pursuit is gone. They lose sight of the beauty, caring heart, and loveliness of their bride that attracted them in the first place.

But it is important for us to notice that there is no hint in this passage that the man is *ever* to stop pursuing his wife. He doesn't finish, get it done, or ever fully accomplish the task of going after his wife. This ongoing pursuit is what we will be referring to as *the Cleaving Principle*.

Once again, we will highlight 4 important points. Today we will begin by focusing on the first one...

1. The marriage relationship requires ongoing, intentional pursuit of the woman, by the man.

God's instruction to the man to pursue the woman must mean that there is something in the pursuit, something that it communicates, that the woman needs to know. When a man pursues his wife consistently, day after day, year after year, she knows in a very special way that he still loves her, still delights in her, and still wants to be with her above all others. When he fails to do so, she may begin to believe that he doesn't care about her, isn't interested in her life, and might even prefer someone else.

Those kinds of doubts become a slow-poison to the relationship... and husbands are responsible to see to it that they are never injected into the marriage relationship in the first place!

Husbands, you need to develop (or re-kindle) a heart that consistently pursues your wife. Here are some ways of looking at this truth that may be helpful...

- Men tend to work at the relationship until it seems to be "*in the bag*" – then they get comfortable and take it for granted. But men, the relationship you have with your wife *needs* constant and continual attention and pursuit.
- Husbands, your wife not only desires for you to want her or to value her...she *needs* it. It is vital that she knows without a doubt that you want her, need her, respect her, and care about her. Doing this nourishes the deepest part of who she is as a woman. God made her to need those things and He made you to provide them!
- Remember also that these types of needs are ones you agreed to meet when you married (remember those wedding vows?). With that in mind, it becomes an issue of being a man of your word. The same "desire" you had then, is to be stoked and kept alive throughout your married life. Getting married was the *first* of many steps of consistent pursuit...
- It is your job, as the husband of your wife, to "win her" again, and again, and again...

Questions for Consideration

- Explain *the Cleaving Principle* in your own words.

- Husbands,what does it do to you to realize that your wife has a need that only you can meet? Wives, what effect does it have on you?

- For both partners: On a 1 to 10 scale (1 = terrible /10 = outstanding) rank the man in your relationship on how he is doing at consistently showing interest in his wife. Take the time over the next few days to discuss how each of you answered this question.

DAY 7

A Prayer Suggestion: Today ask God to open and enliven your heart toward the things you are learning. Set your hope fully on Him to provide the desire and strength to improve and strengthen your marriage.

Genesis 2:24

Therefore a man shall leave his father and his mother and hold fast to his wife, and they shall become one flesh.

Since the concept of *the Cleaving Principle* is still fairly new, let's review it again by recalling the first point we learned yesterday...

1. The marriage relationship requires ongoing, intentional pursuit of the woman, by the man.

It may sound like this principle is entirely dependent on the man. He is the one who has to desire to consistently pursue his wife. He is the one who has to figure out how to chase after her and then actually do it. While all of that is true... there is a responsibility on the part of the wife that we will be addressing today...

2. Wives must *allow* their husbands to consistently pursue them.

You may think that is an odd thing to say, but consider how important a statement it really is. The husband can have an "Ah-ha!" moment and come to realize that he indeed *does* need to consistently chase his wife. He can even begin coming up with ways to do that. But if his wife is resistant toward his pursuit of her, he will not only find it very hard to do so, he will also become discouraged and give up altogether. What are some reasons his wife might not be open to his pursuit?

Hurt or Resentment

It's not uncommon for a wife to feel hurt or resentment because of all the years her husband has *not* pursued her. Even though he may have changed his attitude about the issue now, the hurts from the past don't automatically go away.

What should you do if that is the case? You need to talk it out, and work toward biblical forgiveness. Husband – genuinely repent to your wife; ask her forgiveness. Confess to her every place where you see you've not pursued her as you should. Wife, receive his confession and extend forgiveness.

Many times, this is harder than it sounds. You may need to get help from a mature believer who knows how to help couples resolve conflicts and pursue biblical forgiveness. The wife should also seek to live with her husband in light of the new changes she's beginning to see in his heart. At some point, she needs to give him a chance to prove his new-found commitment in practical ways, in spite of how she feels.

Fear

Another reason that a wife might resist her husband's good-hearted attempts at pursuing her, is that she might be afraid. Perhaps her husband has tried something like this before and didn't follow through. She got her hopes up, only to have them dashed. It would be very natural for her to be afraid of getting her hopes up again.

What should be done? The wife needs to remember

that her faith is ultimately in the Lord, not in her husband. She can give her husband a chance, in obedience to the Lord, trusting Him to work in and through her husband for her good. As she trusts Him, the Lord will enable her to trust her husband, a little bit at a time.

Other helpful tips for the wife...

- Make a point of noticing his efforts, and thanking him for making his commitment toward you practical. All of us are motivated to consistency when we know that our efforts are being noticed!
- Don't cut down or make fun of his efforts at chasing after you, either in private or in public. Consider this: your husband is doing his best to pursue you, just as Christ pursues His church. Be thankful!
- If your husband begins to slack off, don't be afraid to mention it to him, but do so privately and in an encouraging way. For example, you might say, "I know that in your heart you have determined to pursue me more diligently, and I want to encourage you not to give up."
- Finally, if the two of you find some sort of "blockage" with this principle that you can't seem to get around, ask a mature believer or your Pastor for help in determining how you can get around it and move ahead.

Questions for Reflection

For this section of questions, find a time you can sit down together to discuss and analyze your history in this area...

- Husbands, honestly tell your wife how well you think she allows your pursuit of her...

  Examples:

  1. Does she criticize or make fun when you attempt to pursue her?
  2. Does she only recognize when you mess up?
  3. Does she refuse to talk when you initiate conversation?
  4. Does she seem too busy to make time for you?
  5. When you ask her questions about herself or what she's feeling, does she act like or even say, "You should know!" (Wives, your husband doesn't know – that's why he's asking!)
  6. Is your wife staying occupied with "stuff" (computer, hobbies, reading, job, etc.) instead of making room for you?

- Husband, tell your wife where she does a good job at receiving your pursuit. Give examples where you are able.

- Give her some suggestions as to how you'd like her to be more open to your pursuit of her.

- Wives...listen closely, even take notes.

- Wives, ask the Lord to help you to begin applying some of the things your husband suggested.

DAY 8

<u>*A Prayer Suggestion*</u>: Thank God for how He has chased after you. Ask Him to flesh-out that principle between you as husband and wife.

Genesis 2:24

Therefore a man shall leave his father and his mother and hold fast to his wife, and they shall become one flesh.

Today, we are back to *the Cleaving Principle*... and ready to review what we've covered in this section so far...

1. The marriage relationship requires ongoing, intentional pursuit of the woman, by the man.

2. Wives must *allow* their husbands to consistently pursue them.

As we begin today's study, try to think about the last time you learned a new skill or principle. It may have been at work, or in school. As you remember the process you went through, you will probably agree that in every area of learning there are difficult or confusing points that surface from time to time.

The exact same thing is true with the principles we are learning from Genesis 2. Today we are going to address the third point regarding *the Cleaving Principle.* It has to do with the obstacles that block your way.

3. Each partner must diligently and honestly confront the obstacles that stand in the way of *the Cleaving Principle* being applied in your marriage.

Problems/Obstacles

Human nature

Each of us comes into the world with the inherited spiritual characteristics of our ancient ancestors Adam and Eve. Scripture describes this condition by saying that we are all born sinners (Romans 3:10-11). We are not sinners because we sin, we sin because we are sinners. It's part of our nature, part of who we are.

But when we come to faith in Christ all that changes. We become a "new creation" (2 Corinthians 5:17), receiving a new nature from our Savior, Jesus. But we still have a lifetime's worth of old habits and sinful patterns of behavior that we are accustomed to living in. It's these left-over aspects of our original sin nature that can become one of the biggest obstacles we face when seeking to apply a new spiritual truth.

Consider the following ways that our sin nature rears its ugly head...

- Urgency = Action - As a general rule, we only work diligently at things when they seem urgent. Some of you are only doing this study because of urgency. Your relationship hit a crisis moment and you went looking for help. But the fact is that in order for your marriage relationship to be healthy and strong, it has to be diligently maintained, day after day, year after year. Like regular maintenance on your car, *the Cleaving Principle* is about that attitude of ongoing diligence.

- Creatures of Comfort - Another fact of our old patterns of sinful behavior is that we all, to one degree or another, are creatures of comfort and ease. Said another way, we don't naturally sacrifice. We have a bent toward laziness or selfishness. But marriage is a relationship aimed at service to one another. Each of you is to be a primary tool in God's hand to meet the needs and prompt the growth of the other. In order to carry out *the Cleaving Principle* both of you have to intentionally overcome your sinful tendencies toward selfishness.

- Defensiveness - Every one of us tends toward becoming defensive when faced with an issue of our own wrong or neglectful behavior. In short, we often respond in pride, not humility. So men, when your wife points out that you are not chasing her like you used to, it's difficult for you to receive her rebuke – even if it is true. Or ladies, if your husband points out that you used to notice and encourage his efforts at pursuit, but you've slacked off a bit, you may have trouble admitting you're wrong. It goes both ways – pride can be a huge obstacle.

- Our View VS God's View - As an extension of the pride we all struggle with, we often can't submit *our* idea of what is right to *God's* viewpoint. It may be a long-held but wrong belief we are struggling to overcome, or it may be nothing more than the way we were raised. New principles from God's word such as *the Cleaving Principle,* are often difficult for us to resign ourselves to and apply. Work hard in your thoughts and in prayer to get God's mind about this issue. *Ask* the Lord to renew your thinking!

- Hurts from the Past – Being gun-shy is not just for women. Just as it is common for wives to have hurts that keep them from receiving their husband's advances of love, so husbands can feel beaten down and unwilling to try again. Whatever your past, God wants to build a new future for your marriage – and He will only do it through your willing steps of obedience. Husbands, you may need to take a huge step of faith in order to get over this hump. Ask God for strength, get up, brush yourself off, grit your teeth, and try again as you depend on Him. God will honor your reliance on Him to demonstrate the love and interest you need to consistently show your wife.

- Drifting Focus - Finally, in marriage, we are prone to a drifting focus. We begin to think that the issues we are facing are about who is right and who is wrong. But the real issue is not who's right, but what God desires to happen in our marriages. We've got to keep *that* truth in focus.

A Helpful Hint

Husbands, it may be helpful to you if you are able to consider yourself to be like a gardener when it comes to your marriage.

- You are the gardener.
- Your marriage is the garden.
- Your wife is the lovely, beautiful, exquisite, breath-taking, aromatic, vividly stunning flower.
- Your job is to feed, nurture, and care for her (as Jesus does His church).

Questions for Reflection

Today, set aside some time where you can talk together about the truth of *the Cleaving Principle*...

- Consider your own tendencies toward selfishness and pride in light of *the Cleaving Principle*. Ask your spouse for their input. Write down some of the things you'd like to see change in your own character and behavior.

- Discuss ways that each of you can work to affirm and encourage the other in the areas of weakness you've discussed.

- Pray together, for the things each of you has admitted. This is not a time to bash each other, but a time to support and encourage each other as you both go to the Lord for help.

DAY 9

<u>*A Prayer Suggestion*</u>: Ask God to use today's time with Him to open your understanding in a deeper way. Ask Him to show you what you may be misunderstanding about *the Cleaving Principle*, and to clarify it for you.

Genesis 2:24

Therefore a man shall leave his father and his mother and hold fast to his wife, and they shall become one flesh.

As we get started today, we'll once again review the main points we've covered so far in *the Cleaving Principle*...

1. The marriage relationship requires ongoing, intentional pursuit of the woman, by the man.

2. Wives must *allow* their husbands to consistently pursue them.

3. Each partner must diligently and honestly confront the obstacles that stand in the way of *the Cleaving Principle* being applied in your marriage.

By now I hope that you have a pretty clear idea of what *the Cleaving Principle* is, and why it is important. But it's possible that you have developed some misconceptions about it. Today we'll address that issue...

4. Misconceptions in how you apply *the Cleaving Principle* can cause great harm to be done.

Fire is a good thing. It can cook your food, warm your home, or provide light to a dark room. But if fire is allowed outside the fireplace, away from the stove, or out of the lantern, it can wreak havoc! In the same way, *the Cleaving Principle* is a wonderful concept that can be very helpful in the strengthening of your marriage. But if you misunderstand it and apply it wrongly, it can cause a great deal of hurt.

Misconception #1 –Positive events, experiences, or gifts fuel the relationship for the long term.

A gift of flowers – an anniversary trip together – working through a difficult time side by side – all of these are wonderful opportunities to build unity and strength into your marriage. But you are misguided if you believe that those types of things can carry the relationship for very long. They are good while they last, but the truth is that they don't last very long at all. Consistent effort at keeping up "the chase" is required in every marriage relationship. Consistency over the long haul is vital!

Misconception # 2 – If I have married the right person, the feelings of love, affection, and devotion should come automatically or naturally.

We've all had that fluttery feeling in our stomach when we are around that "special someone." It's part of the way courtship and romantic relationships work themselves out. But many of us have been sold a "bill of goods" by our culture, and believe that those feelings are the main barometer of whether a relationship is meant to be or not. Feelings, while a great icing on the cake of marriage, are not the main ingredient. They can come and go, and can even grow over time as each partner does their part in following God's instructions for marriage.

Let us say it another way. There will be times when you have to apply *the Cleaving Principle* and other things you learn in this study, even when you don't feel like it. Marriage is not an emotional wonderland where no bad feelings ever arise. It's a relationship of love, a commitment you've made to care for each other no matter what. That includes both the presence and absence of feelings.

Misconception #3 - If a husband's emotions change at any point (toward his spouse or because of circumstances), it's "OK" not to pursue her.

Again, emotions are not the main gauge of your relationship, commitment is. Not only is it a commitment to your wife, but it is also a commitment you have made before the Lord. Don't let the fleeting nature of emotions convince you that your responsibility to chase after your wife can wane. She needs what you have to give, and your pursuit of her is what opens the door to meeting that need! And it's under the influence of that kind of love that she will best grow and blossom!

Misconception #4 – Husbands are justified in not pursuing their wife if they think she is not doing her part.

Marriage does take two people– there is no doubt about that. But more importantly, it takes two people who are each committed to doing their own part, regardless of what the other is or is not doing. Your responsibility, whether husband or wife, is to obey God in how you carry out your role in your marriage. It's really that simple.

My wife has often helped couples understand this truth by sharing the following illustration. Imagine yourself, after this life is over, standing before God to give an account of your life. He points out that you were not fully committed to doing everything you needed to do for the sake of your marriage.

When He asks you why you didn't give your all for your marriage, what will you say? Do you think He'll be O.K. with an answer like this? "Well, she didn't do her part, so I figured I'd do the same." It's ridiculous even to consider. God will hold each of us responsible for our lives and commitments, completely independent of those around us. Our obedience to Him is *our* obedience to Him – and we are responsible for it.

Questions for Reflection

As in the previous few days, set aside time to walk through the following questions together... Remember, honesty is mandatory and defensiveness is not allowed. Your goal here is to discover things that are short-circuiting your relationship – and to do it together, as a team.

While there may be some difficult things to say, or hear, trust the Lord to help you deal with the reality of your relationship, and move it beyond those things!

- Wives, honestly tell your husband how well you feel that he pursues you...

<u>Examples</u>:

1. Does he initiate time together?
2. Does he share his thoughts and feelings with you freely?
3. Does he sacrifice time or other things in order to be with you?
4. Does he remember special days, etc.?
5. Does he affirm you with his words, regularly (I love you, I appreciate you, I like being with you, You make me so happy, I'm proud of you, etc.)
6. Does he show interest in the things that make up your life?

- Wives give your husband some suggestions as to how you'd like him to pursue or show interest in you.

- Husbands...listen closely, even take notes.

- Husbands, ask the Lord to help you to begin applying some of the things your wife suggested.

DAY 10

<u>*A Prayer Suggestion*</u>: Thank the Lord for everything you are learning, and for the way in which He is teaching you. Ask Him to protect and preserve your marriage relationship as you struggle through some potentially difficult areas.

Genesis 2:24

Therefore a man shall leave his father and his mother and hold fast to his wife, and they shall become one flesh.

In this last lesson for this chapter, we will review what has been taught so that you have another opportunity to meditate on the truths you've learned. The following four points are vital to a good understanding of *the Cleaving Principle*...

1. The marriage relationship requires ongoing pursuit of the woman, by the man.

2. Wives must *allow* their husbands to consistently pursue them.

3. Each partner must diligently and honestly confront the obstacles that stand in the way of *the Cleaving Principle* being applied in your marriage.

4. Misconceptions in how you apply *the Cleaving Principle* can cause great harm to be done.

The Cleaving Principle is a powerful concept that is able to help you build delight and real joy into your marriage relationship. But it only works as both of you are faithful to do what is necessary to carry it to fruition.

If you are the husband, set your mind to chase after your wife, intentionally finding ways to express to her how much she means to you. If time, disappointment, or hurt have blocked your ability to even desire to chase her, sincerely ask the Lord to renew your love for your wife – and watch for Him to begin doing it!

If you are the wife, learn to receive the efforts your husband is making to pursue you, without sarcasm, skepticism, or resentment. Continue to talk through the hurts that make it difficult for you to really believe that he wants to pursue you.

Through the proper application of this principle, you can find a renewed joy in your relationship that you never knew could be possible!

Questions for Reflection

- How would you describe *the Cleaving Principle* in your own words, and why it is important?
- Which of the 4 main points above stand out to you the most? Why do you think this is?
- When it comes to proving your commitment to carrying out *the Cleaving Principle*, do you see any things that you particularly need to adjust? What are they?
- What do you think it will take for you to actually do what you need to do, instead of just having a good intention about it?

SECTION THREE

3

The Unity Principle

DAY 11

<u>A Prayer Suggestion</u>: Take some time to quiet yourself and prepare for whatever God has in store for you in today's lesson.

Genesis 2:24

Therefore a man shall leave his father and his mother and hold fast to his wife, and they shall become one flesh.

It is truly amazing how full of meaning God's word is. We have been two weeks on this one verse, Genesis 2:24 and still are not finished with the principles it has to teach us. Notice the last line of the verse, "*and they shall become one flesh.*" It's this "*one flesh*" principle we are going to be focusing on this week – and we will be referring to it as *the Unity Principle.*

What God is telling us in this phrase is one aspect of what *he* intends marriage to be. It is a coming together of a man and a woman, each bearing the image of their Creator, to become one. It's a paradox, a mystery – how two individuals can become "one" in marriage – and yet still be individuals.

Clearly, neither of them is absorbed into the other. Yet, God says they are "*one flesh*" when they are married. What He is telling us is that a marriage relationship is intended to *unify* the husband and wife. This week we will be exploring different aspects of that unity. The main implication of this Unity Principle is this:

Marriage is a *total union* of two people – in every area of life.

Think about your life as a bookshelf with many different compartments built into it. Each of these compartments represents different "areas" of your life. On the shelf you can find compartments labeled entertainment, finances, family, work, hobbies, church life, etc.

While many of those areas may be things that you do all on your own (like work), they are still areas that can and should be shared with your spouse so that you can be better unified in your marriage. You are better able to be on the same page with your spouse when you are sharing information and insights about the various areas you each experience. Let's consider some examples...

Hobbies

Let's suppose there is a husband who very much enjoys fishing, hunting, camping, etc. He likes to do those things any chance he gets. *The Unity Principle* requires that he discuss his participation in those activities with his wife – before making plans! Let's take a few moments to clarify what is behind this idea...

- In this scenario the man is *not* talking to his wife before making plans in order to get ***permission*** to do what he's wanting...
- He is talking with his wife first ***out of consideration*** *for their unity as a couple*.
- The husband in this scenario would want to submit his own desires and plans to the good of their mutual relationship and its needs.
- The same would hold true if it were the wife who were wanting to make plans for herself.
- The conversations the couple has about these kinds of issues are done out of respect for each other and for the marriage.

Church life

The leadership at church has begun to promote a fabulous new study that will be taking place on Sunday evenings. The wife hears about it and thinks it would be a great thing for she and her husband to join. Her assumption is that her husband would be as excited about the study as she is, so she signs them up to be participants. In this scenario, the wife did not consider *the Unity Principle*. What should she have done?

- Most likely, she believed that this study would be very beneficial for both her and her husband, but out of consideration for the unity of their relationship, she should have talked about it with her husband before making any commitments.
- By checking with him in a situation like this, the two of them have the opportunity to communicate about what is happening in each of their lives, and whether or not there is sufficient time, personal energy, and resources to be involved. This gives them the opportunity to be unified in their decision.

Work

The husband has just been informed by his boss that he is going to have to work late. The problem is that he and his wife had planned to spend the evening talking about whether or not to purchase a new vehicle. In light of *the Unity Principle*, what should he do?

- Again, consideration of their unity as a couple is of first importance, even over the demands of the job.
- There are many ways the husband could approach this issue...

1. He could call his wife to explain the situation and discover together if there is another time in the near future when they can have their discussion about a new vehicle. If so, they should solidify those plans immediately so that other things don't creep in and rob them of that time.
2. Depending on the specifics of the circumstance, he might feel that the commitment he has already made to his wife is more important than the extra work hours. In this case he would have to tactfully let his boss know that he already had plans for the evening and simply cannot stay past his normal time.

- Things he should *not* do in light of *the Unity Principle*...
    1. Stay late at work without any communication about the situation.
    2. Assume that his wife will be fine with whatever decision he makes. Even if she is, *the Unity Principle* requires that he consider her enough to initiate communication.

If we could boil this principle down into one easy-to-understand word – it would be "*consideration*." Each partner is mindful of actively considering the other, no matter the circumstance. This simple act helps to foster and preserve the unity of their relationship.

Questions for Reflection

In today's questions, try to avoid thinking about how your spouse needs to improve. Instead, focus on how YOU need to improve. Be honest and let the Holy Spirit guide you to see what is true...

- Write out your understanding of *the Unity Principle*...

- Write down how you see this principle being important to the health and stability of your marriage relationship.

- Put yourself in each of the examples listed above. Modify it to fit the details of your life. In the past, how have you done at considering the unity of your relationship with your spouse? (a 1 to 10 scale might be helpful).

- Carefully consider the ways you see yourself falling short. Ask the Lord for His help in making a stronger commitment toward unity in your marriage, and for wisdom in applying what you have learned.

SECTION THREE:
The Unity Principle

DAY 12

<u>A Prayer Suggestion</u>: Ask the Lord to do supernatural things to facilitate a greater sense of unity between you and your spouse as you endeavor to do your part in applying what you are learning.

Genesis 2:24

Therefore a man shall leave his father and his mother and hold fast to his wife, and they shall become one flesh.

The last study introduced what we are referring to as *the Unity Principle*. Simply stated, it is that:

Marriage is a *total union* of two people – in every area of life.

Today we are going to consider one aspect of this definition - *total union*. It doesn't take much thought to realize - that's a huge goal! When God brings a man and woman together in marriage, He does not expect for them to be roommates, or simply partners. He intends for them to move into a relationship of unity that they have never before experienced.

This total union is how God ensures that each of them is loved and cared for. He places them in a relationship with a partner who has just as much invested in the relationship as they do. They are one... so what is beneficial to one of them is beneficial to the other.

Beautiful truths about *the Unity Principle*

An attitude of oneness

- It's hard work to change your mindset from independent and self-centered to one of constant consideration and care for another person.
- Each partner should make the development of this attitude a conscious and intentional goal – leaning on the Lord for His help in doing so.
- You may need to make a "project" of this – taking intentional steps to "*renew your mind*" (Romans 12:2) along these lines day after day. Perhaps a note card with *the Unity Principle* written on it would be helpful. Throughout the day, you can take it out and pray over it... asking the Lord to help you become more mindful of the need to be unified with your spouse.

Teamwork & togetherness

The Unity Principle facilitates a sense of teamwork, and togetherness. There are many words to describe it:

- family
- partnership
- connection
- support
- cooperation
- affirmation
- friendship
- oneness

Trust, intimacy, fulfillment

Total sharing, as *the Unity Principle* encourages, ultimately brings fulfillment in marriage. Anytime you see a marriage where the partners are unified as a couple, you'll find that overall they are happy, content, encouraged, and healthy people.

Questions for Reflection

- On a scale of 1 to 10 (1 = "not possible" and 10 = "entirely possible"), write down how possible you think it is for a couple to really be totally unified.

- On a scale of 1 to 10 (1 = "not possible" and 10 = "entirely possible"), write down how possible you think ***God*** believes it is for a couple to be totally unified. Consider Luke 1:35-37 before you answer.

- What do you think may be contributing to the doubts you have about whether or not your marriage relationship can experience this kind of unity?

- Spend some time in prayer, asking God to do *His* will in this area – to teach you and your spouse how to move closer and closer to a place of complete unity. Ask Him to supernaturally overcome the obstacles that you see, as well as the ones that you don't see.

DAY 13

A Prayer Suggestion: Take a few moments to ask the Lord to remind you of *His* heart for your marriage relationship. Ask Him to make your marriage healthy, strong, and full of His presence.

Genesis 2:24

Therefore a man shall leave his father and his mother and hold fast to his wife, and they shall become one flesh.

This week we are considering another of God's principles for marriage found in Genesis 2:24. We are referring to it as *the Unity Principle*. Again, *the Unity Principle* is that:

> **Marriage is a *total union* of two people – in every area of life.**

Today we are going to focus on another aspect of the definition - *every area of life*.– To say that a marriage is to be a union of two people in "every area of life" is to make a pretty broad statement, isn't it? It doesn't just include most things – it includes everything! Our lesson today will explore one of the main areas where couples oftentimes have trouble in working toward and being unified completely.

Ownership or Custody issues

When two people get married, they are literally combining two different worlds, two different histories. Each of them has their own way of looking at life, their own way of dealing with situations, their own areas of responsibility, their own financial obligations, their own possessions, their own family relationships, and many other things that are theirs alone. These things come from family and relational experiences, learned behaviors and concepts, and habits that are unique to each one of them.

But when they get married, all of that needs to change. The two are no longer separate – God says they are to be "*one*." Today we are going to consider how this relates to the joint-custody of property, money, and other resources.

Biblically, when a man and woman become a married couple, everything that was previously owned, controlled, managed, or used by *one* person, has transferred into the custody of *two* people.

This will require a great deal of communication, beginning from the start of the marriage. Some of the things that will need to be discussed are:

- How each of you views stewardship (the management of the things God has given you) – for property, money, time, etc.
- How are you going to bring your two differing views to a place of unity? Sometimes this will be easy, but other times it will be extremely difficult.

Anything that is *not* submitted to mutual ownership and control will inevitably lead to conflict and problems in the marriage. This could occur in many areas...

- Possessions
- Money/investments
- Holiday plans/traditions
- Children from previous relationships
- Your own bodies – (1 Corinthians 7:4)

If either of you withholds mutual custody of anything you possess, your relationship *will be* damaged in terms of trust and intimacy. Questions and doubts will begin to surface...

- Doesn't he trust me?
- Why won't she allow me to be a part of that? Does she think I'm stupid or incapable?
- I can't feel very close to him when he won't let me be a part of his life.
- She doesn't really care what I think about that situation, so why should I even bother?

Practical Issues

- For the reasons listed above, it's not best for couples to have separate bank accounts, or "his money" and "her money." You are now *one*, and should live in that way in everything. This doesn't mean each of you should not have personal spending money figured into the budget – but it does mean that you will agree together on what those amounts should be.
- When a new marriage involves children from a previous marriage, the biological parent should work extra hard to include and affirm their new spouse as the children's parent. You may have to work very slowly, but you should make sure you are working *together* in regard to household rules, behavior, and consequences, with no thought of, "they are my kids, not yours."
- As well, the non-biological parent will need the children's biological parent to insist that the children honor and respect their "new" parent, as the Bible teaches.
- Major purchases should only be made when sufficient discussion, financial consideration, and prayer have

taken place between you, *as a couple*. A shared decision is of great importance for the sake of unity.

- When you fail to address these kinds of issues in a unified way, there is a great possibility of anger, resentment, bitterness, and conflict taking root in your marriage. It's better to do the hard work needed to prevent such things and keep your relationship healthy.

Questions for Reflection

- In reading through this section, what things about *your* relationship have come to mind that you know need to be discussed.

- Take some time to make a list of those things, describing what it is about each one that you believe needs to be ironed out or adjusted.

- Talk to your spouse and set aside time for the two of you to talk about those things. Remember to invite the Lord into the process... He is eager to help!

DAY 14

<u>*A Prayer Suggestion*</u>*:* Ask the Lord to open your heart to Him in greater ways today. Ask Him to show you how you can better apply this *Unity Principle* or actively remove barriers to it that exist in your own heart.

Genesis 2:24

Therefore a man shall leave his father and his mother and hold fast to his wife, and they shall become one flesh.

Quickly, in review – remind yourself what we mean when we speak of *the Unity Principle* as seen in Genesis 2:24...

> **Marriage is a *total union* of two people – in every area of life.**

This is God's desire for every married couple. The imagery the Lord uses can't be more clear! He calls us "*one flesh*" as a married couple. Think that through for a moment. The reality is that even after marriage, you are two separate people. You each have your own personality, desires, and physical bodies. *Yet*, God Himself says that you are to be "*one flesh*" - as if your very bodies were one.

Admittedly, this could be a veiled reference to the physical relationship that occurs between husband and wife in the physical consummation of their marriage... but contextually it points to something more. This idea of becoming "*one flesh*" is in contrast to what was true before the marriage took place, when each partner lived with their mother and father. They were each individuals, living in a household with a couple (mother and father) who had become one. Now that they are married, they are to live as one with their new spouse.

Obstacles to Total Unity

Once again, the task of becoming *"one flesh"* is hindered by many obstacles – things that make a unified relationship more difficult to achieve. In today's lesson we'll be considering *some* of the more common barriers to a one flesh relationship between husband and wife. Though these are not in any way all of the things that can disrupt *the Unity Principle*, they are some of the most common...

Dominance Issues

A tragic situation which is all too common in marriages is that one of the partners takes on a posture of dominance over the other. What we are addressing here has nothing to do with leadership; the Bible affirms that leadership is a very necessary and vital role in the marriage relationship. We are talking about dominance. Perhaps a definition would be helpful...

DOMINANT – *ruling; controlling*

A person who is dominant has a tendency to rule or control the other person. It's the exact opposite of total unity because the one in control is not interested in working together. Instead that person wants to be in and remain in, control. If there is a person who is dominant in a marriage relationship, they can be spotted by their attitudes and actions...

- Inconsiderate / self-absorbed
- Arrogant / bossy
- Demanding / selfish
- Expects others to do what he/she says or expects
- May be an "emotional terrorist" - in other words, this person may often have emotional outbursts to get their way, influence a decision, or cause the other person to back down. This may include violence, extreme anger, or fits of tears.

As you can see, when one person in a marriage exerts dominance over the other, *the Unity Principle* is not able to be practiced. To overcome this destructive pattern of behavior, some very difficult but important steps need to be taken...like a teeter-totter, someone has to upset the balance in order to see a change take place... and it may not be an easy or short process!

1. *First, prayer should be top on the list.* Only God can effectively and lastingly remove such long-standing patterns of aggressive or manipulative behavior in a person.
2. Next, *the domineering behavior needs to be addressed*. Do this carefully, lovingly, and calmly... and don't let yourself back down. You have to love your spouse enough to help them with this dangerous and harmful habit.

If the dominant person sees his/her wrong – then praise the Lord! He has already gotten you through the first and perhaps the most difficult step!

- In such a case, the dominant person must intentionally "step down," humbling themselves by admitting their wrong to their spouse, asking them for forgiveness, and seeking the Lord to help them overcome their bad habit.
- They must also work extra hard at consideration of their spouse, learning to work together in the relationship as "*one*."
- In almost every case, it will be helpful to find someone well-versed in these kinds of relational issues who can help you with the practical challenges that will arise as you try to make these important changes.

If the dominant person is unable or unwilling to see or admit their wrong, then the person who is being mistreated must do a very hard thing... they must "step up" and confront the behavior as it occurs.

- You will be guided best and with the most clarity by intentionally bringing the Lord into each situation. What I means is this: the confronting spouse must raise their concerns in light of what God thinks about the behavior and what kind of behavior He desires instead.
- There are situations where such confrontation may result in a violent reaction from the dominant spouse. Such situations should be approached with much prayer and wisdom... and perhaps with outside help.

Issues Involving the Distant Past

In many marriages, one or both of the partners may come from a background that included abuse, betrayal, or other extremely hurtful rejections. In such a case it will be very natural for that person to have a difficult time trusting. This would be true with their spouse, perhaps even more than with others due to the intimate nature of the relationship. Such issues are very difficult, but must be addressed in order for *the Unity Principle* to become a reality in their marriage. Some thoughts to consider...

- The spouse who is having trouble trusting probably has trouble trusting God too. You can see that this is a spiritual issue as much as it is anything else.
- While the hurts that have occurred in the past are very real, the underlying issue is pride. The person who has been hurt is in a self-protective mode, thinking only of themselves. It is vital that they learn to step out in acts of trust, obedience, and love toward their spouse.
- If you find your spouse being distrustful because of such issues, it may encourage you to know that God will oftentimes use you, the spouse of a hurt individual as the one to help them overcome their fear and distrust. As you love your spouse sacrificially and in a long-suffering manner, he/she will begin to see what God's unconditional love is like, and begin learning to trust Him... and you.

Unresolved Conflicts

All married couples experience conflict with each other. But not all married couples know how to work out those conflicts in a biblical way. Put yourself in this scenario... an argument erupts. You disagree with each other strongly. Hurtful things are said by each of you, and you finally go your separate ways to cool down. Over the next couple of days the feelings subside a bit, and you begin to relate as if nothing has happened. You may even begin to feel like it wasn't such a big deal after all and that you should "let it go."

It may *feel* that way, but that isn't the truth. The fact is that wrong was done. Each of you said things that were hurtful or cruel toward the other. Each of you responded out of hurt rather than out of love.

Those unresolved, painful issues *will* come back to your mind, and the hurt *will* resurface again..if the wrongs that were done are not made right through the biblical pattern of reconciliation. They will linger under the surface of your relationship and begin to fester. Resentment or bitterness will eventually set-in, and the only logical result is that you will separate from each other on various levels... in direct opposition to *the Unity Principle*. Over time, the consequences of such left-over hurts can be catastrophic.

Some points to consider...

- Things that are under the surface need to be exposed. Like an infection in a cut, they will fester and become inflamed over time, causing great pain, resentment, and disunity in your marriage.
- The one who has been hurt needs to be able to express the degree to which they were hurt. This is the process of "*going to your brother*" who has sinned against you (Matthew 18:15).
- The one who is being confronted must *humbly* accept that they have done wrong – confess their wrong to the other, and repent of it, asking forgiveness.
- The one who has been hurt, in light of God's forgiveness of them, must forgive when asked (Matthew 6:15).
- Often, couples are unable to get to the bottom of offenses that have existed for many years without help from another mature believer who understands this process of confession, repentance, and forgiveness.

Questions for Reflection

- Would you like to experience this kind of "*oneness*" in your marriage? Does it seem too good to be true?

- Of the 3 types of obstacles listed, which do you feel is the most applicable to your marriage situation? Check with your spouse to see if they feel the same way.

- It is not impossible, but it is unusual for a couple to be objective enough about themselves to resolve these kinds of issues on their own. Set aside a time together to discuss what you believe you need to resolve and whether you would like to seek help as you walk through that process.

DAY 15

A Prayer Suggestion: Consider the Lord's presence with you today. He has promised to be with you through His Holy Spirit, as your Guide, Teacher, and Counselor. Ask Him to lead you today.

Genesis 2:24

Therefore a man shall leave his father and his mother and hold fast to his wife, and they shall become one flesh.

This is the final day for us to consider *the Unity Principle* in depth.

Marriage is a *total union* of two people – in every area of life.

One last thing to consider is this... Marriages in our day and age are hurting. The divorce rate continues to climb. Domestic abuse is on the rise. Even in the church those who are giving up on their marriages is almost equal to the rate of those outside the church.

What could be more needed than couples who are equipped and able to set a good example of what marriage is supposed to be? Their example, their love for each other, their unity – could be the catalyst that many struggling couples need in order to believe that there is hope for *their* marriage.

You could be one of those examples that turn somebody around. The impact of a godly marriage that is living out *the Unity Principle* could be very powerful!

You may think that you are nowhere near being ready to set an example for others to follow... and you may be right. But because of your willingness to complete this marriage improvement project you are already far ahead of most couples when it comes to working toward a healthy and strong marriage. It is only a matter of time, your obedience, and God's faithfulness until you are ready to begin leading others to a healthier place in their marriages.

- Keep your heart open to the Lord as you continue this process. He will be faithful to guide you as you are faithful to listen to His leading.
- Continue to fight the battle to overcome your old habits toward independence. *The Unity Principle* will only benefit your marriage as your independence is replaced with partnership.
- Make your marriage a matter of daily prayer. As you pray for your marriage, the Lord will give you a greater desire and personal willingness to see it become all He desires it to be.

Questions for Reflection

- How often do you pray for your marriage? Take a little time right now to do that!

- Do you feel that you and your spouse are united in wanting your marriage to grow and become more healthy? Talk and pray about this issue together.

- In your own words, recap why *the Unity Principle* is so important to your marriage.

- Talk with your spouse about your commitment to this process. Perhaps you could write it down together, sign it, and put it in your house someplace where you would see it often.

SECTION FOUR

4

Communication Is Key

DAY 16

A Prayer Suggestion: Spend a few moments in quiet before the Lord. Ask Him to open your heart to the realities (painful or joyful) about your marriage. Ask Him to guide you toward understanding as you begin to look at the issue of communication in your marriage.

We live in a world where communication devices are common to us all. Television, cell phones, texting, email, blogging, chat, social networking websites, and Internet newsgroups are some of the newest modes of communication, not to mention the good old reliable telephone and postal mail!

With all these technological advances, you would think that our culture would become *better* at effective communication, but the reality is that we've actually gotten worse at it! It's not worse because we don't have enough *ways* to communicate, but because we still don't understand what true communication really *is*.

There are many passages of scripture that teach us about various aspects of communication, but today we'll center our thoughts around two different scriptures – one that focuses on the speaking part of communication, and another that focuses on the listening... check them out...

Ephesians 4:29 *Let no corrupting talk come out of your mouths, but only such as is good for building up, as fits the occasion, that it may give grace to those who hear.*

Proverbs 1:5 *Let the wise hear and increase in learning, and the one who understands obtain guidance.*

This week, as we focus on what the scriptures say about communication, we'll apply those principles specifically to your marriage relationship. There's no better place to begin than to clarify what really takes place when communication happens.

Defining Communication

In the following definition of communication, notice the underlined words, and consider their importance as they are discussed below...

> *Definition*: Communication is a *process* of sharing information (thoughts, opinions, emotions, etc.) in a verbal or non-verbal way that includes *talking* and *listening*, resulting in *understanding*.

1. It is a **process**.

   In other words – good communication takes *time*! You can't expect effective and meaningful communication to take place in the brief moments when you are passing each other during the day. You have to allow and make time for good communication if it is going to happen.

2. It includes **talking.**

   This may sound incredibly obvious, but it needs to be said. Why? Because many people have grown up in homes where even simple conversation was non-existent. As a result, they many not know *how* to talk in a meaningful way. Or, they may be in a very bad habit of simply not talking. Talking together is essential for effective communication to take place, and though it may be intimidating for some, it can be learned and mastered!

3. It includes **listening**.

   Real listening is more than simply having sound waves bounce off your eardrums. It is a *desire to understand* what your spouse is saying. Said another way, if you aren't interested in what is being said, you will stop listening.

4. It results in **understanding**.

   When you really understand your spouse, you begin to experience a wonderful gift from the Lord - the ability to live together in a compassionate, sensitive, loving, and Christ-like way.

In the remainder of this lesson we will begin to consider the first of these important components of communication -*it is a process.*

The process of communication

Our family was blessed for 4 years to live in the state of Hawaii (you know, somebody's got to do it!). The Hawaiian Islands are known world-wide to have some of the clearest, most beautiful blue waters anywhere in the world. But in the wintertime, those beautiful blue waters transform into some of the largest, most dangerous waves on the planet!

All winter long the waves crash in a deafening roar along the northern shorelines, many times 30 to 60 feet in height! When winter is over, the waves begin to return to their normal, peaceful patterns.

But though the waves return to normal size, it may be months before the waters return to their usual clarity. The churning waves of the winter months stirred up all kinds of sand, silt, debris, and rocks that require time to settle to the ocean floor.

This is a very fitting analogy of the process that is required for good communication to happen. Just as the Hawaiian waters require time to become clear after the winter waves, clarity and understanding in communication require time as well.

The first words that are said about any subject, especially one that is touchy or difficult, are seldom a clear picture of what the person really means. Those first words are introductory in nature, opening up the topic and making the other person aware of their desire to discuss the issue.

As the two of them express their thoughts and feelings about the subject, back and forth through the course of the conversation, the clock is ticking...and the process of communication has begun.

Seldom can clarity come in a few moments of interaction because of the differences in perception, thinking, world-view, and emotions that each of the people in the conversation brings into the dialogue. Over time, as each is working to hear and understand the other, communication happens and clarity comes.

Questions for Reflection

- Explain in your own words why communication *has* to be a process...

- Have you ever found yourself becoming impatient with the process that good communication requires? In light of what you've learned today, why do you think that is?

- Do you ever feel frustrated with your spouse because they seem to be slow at understanding what you are saying? What light does today's lesson shed on that frustration?

DAY 17

A Prayer Suggestion: Ask the Lord to give you a greater understanding of the type of effort you need to put into good communication, so that your marriage can be stronger and healthier. Ask Him to equip you to do what you need to do.

In the previous lesson, we defined communication by focusing on 4 components that make it work. Before we move ahead with today's lesson, let's review the definition...

Definition: Communication is a *process* (verbal and non-verbal) of sharing information (thoughts, opinions, emotions, etc.) that includes *talking* and *listening*, resulting in *understanding*.

We already looked at the first part of the definition...it's a process. Today we will consider the next one – *talking*.

Talking

The Bible has a great deal to say about how we talk and the role that talking should play in our lives as believers. Take your time as you read the passages below and consider what they might mean for you (resist the temptation to apply them to your spouse. Do work on *you* right now...)

Proverbs 10:19 – *When words are many, transgression is not lacking, but whoever restrains his lips is prudent.*

The point of this passage is *not* that we should avoid talking because it might lead to sin. The point is that we have to be careful with our words. We need to be wise in how we use them, making sure to allow others room to communicate their thoughts as needed.

> ***Proverbs 15:2*** *– The tongue of the wise commends knowledge, but the mouths of fools pour out folly.*

Here we find a contrast in how a wise person and a foolish person communicate. The wise person is prone to communicate in a way as that benefits those who are listening. He works to facilitate understanding or knowledge. The foolish person will speak silly, unhelpful, or harmful things that make things worse!

> ***Proverbs 18:13*** *– If one gives an answer before he hears, it is his folly and shame.*

One of the keys to effective communication is to really *hear* what the others in the conversation are saying. That means that sometimes we have to keep our mouths shut and work at listening. The scriptures characterize us as "*foolish*" if we speak before we really understand what it is that we are talking about! Does that sound familiar at all?

> ***Proverbs 29:20*** *– Do you see a man who is hasty in his words? There is more hope for a fool than for him.*

All of us have been hasty in what we've said from time to time. In pointing that out, the scriptures are not teaching us that communication is hopeless for us, but it is warning us that we have our work cut out for us! It is our responsibility before God to learn self-discipline when it comes to our speech.

Ephesians 4:29 – *Let no corrupting talk come out of your mouths, but only such as is good for building up, as fits the occasion, that it may give grace to those who hear.*

Clearly we are responsible for what we say. God expects us to use our words to benefit those who hear them. That alone rules out much of what we could say (course jokes, sarcastic jabs, intentionally hurtful or demeaning statements, etc.) God holds us accountable for the *way* in which we use our words!

James 3:2-12 - *For we all stumble in many ways. And if anyone does not stumble in what he says, he is a perfect man, able also to bridle his whole body. If we put bits into the mouths of horses so that they obey us, we guide their whole bodies as well. Look at the ships also: though they are so large and are driven by strong winds, they are guided by a very small rudder wherever the will of the pilot directs. So also the tongue is a small member, yet it boasts of great things. How great a forest is set ablaze by such a small fire! And the tongue is a fire, a world of unrighteousness. The tongue is set among our members, staining the whole body, setting on fire the entire course of life, and set on fire by hell. For every kind of beast and bird, of reptile and sea creature, can be tamed and has been tamed by mankind, but no human being can tame the tongue. It is a restless evil, full of deadly poison. With it we bless our Lord and Father, and with it we curse people who are made in the likeness of God. From the same mouth come blessing and cursing. My brothers, these things ought not to be so. Does a spring pour forth from the same opening both fresh and salt water? Can a fig tree, my brothers, bear olives, or a grapevine produce figs? Neither can a salt pond yield fresh water.*

James is not trying to discourage us from all conversation, he's wanting to make us painfully aware of the potential for hypocrisy and evil that exists in our speech. His desire is that we Christians speak in ways that bring honor, instead of shame, to Jesus.

There are many more passages that teach us about the proper and godly use of the tongue. But these are sufficient for now to show us that we are responsible to communicate in ways that are glorifying to God and helpful to those who hear!

When we apply this to the marriage relationship and the communication that must happen in order for it to be and remain healthy, we can see that godly talking is an essential part of that process. Consider these thoughts...

- The only way your spouse will know what you are thinking or feeling is by you talking to them. Your spouse is *not* a mind reader.
- Work hard to keep your cool as you talk together. Many offenses come from misunderstandings rather than intentional slights or jabs. Learn to ask questions to clarify what your spouse is saying before you get upset. You might find there is nothing to be upset about!
- Even if your spouse says something intentionally hurtful to you, the old saying is still true: two wrongs don't make a right! God expects *you* to obey Him when it comes to how you respond to your spouse.
- If your spouse has a hard time talking, or needs to think for a bit before responding, trust the Spirit to enable you to be patient. Patience, humility, and understanding of their struggle will help them gain freedom and confidence in talking to you.
- Learn to let your spouse talk – without interrupting them. You need to hear all of what they have to say if you are going to have a chance of understanding them.

- Genuine, honest, and caring questions are your ally. They will enable your spouse to better express themselves and will enable you to understand them to a greater degree. But be careful that your questions are posed in a way that expresses interest, not interrogation!

Finally, consider how conversation is like a tennis match. One person hits the ball over the net toward the other person. Their job is to hit the ball back. A conversation is the same way. Both partners need to talk, in turn, and in response to what has been said to them. As each does this with a genuine desire to understand the other, communication begins to happen.

Questions for Reflection

Do your best to answer these for yourself, not for your spouse...

- On a scale of 1 to 10 (1 = terrible, 10 = terrific) where would you rate yourself in terms of being *willing* to honestly and lovingly talk with your spouse.

- On a scale of 1 to 10 (1 = terrible, 10 = terrific) where would you rate yourself in terms of *actually talking* in an honest and loving way?

- Takes some time together to discuss your answers to these two questions with your spouse. Look at how he/she answered. Are you both willing to work at good communication (1st question) ? How well are each of you doing at that right now (2nd question)?

- Pray together, asking the Lord to increase your willingness *and* ability to communicate in healthy and important ways.

DAY 18

A Prayer Suggestion: Ask the Lord to make you a good listener. Consider how important it is for you to *really* listen. Ask the Lord to show you those things during today's lesson!

We've already considered a good definition of communication and have begun exploring the part talking plays in that definition. Before we move ahead with today's lesson, let's review the definition...

Definition: Communication is a *process* (verbal and non-verbal) of sharing information (thoughts, opinions, emotions, etc.) that includes *talking* and *listening*, resulting in *understanding*.

Today we will consider two more aspects of good communication – *listening* and *understanding*.

Listening

James 1:19-20 – *Know this, my beloved brothers: let every person be quick to hear, slow to speak, slow to anger; for the anger of man does not produce the righteousness of God.*

As we understood from the last lesson, talking is very important. Without it there is very little communication that can happen. But for most of us, the problem is not that we talk too little, but rather that we talk too much! This passage prescribes listening (*quick to hear*) as one of the most important components of communication. Notice the comparison between speaking and listening. We are to be "*quick*" to listen, but "*slow*" to speak. In God's mind, the priority in any communication is to *truly listen* to the person you are speaking with.

Points to Consider

- Too often our desire is to be *heard* – when we really need to focus on listening. There is truly no other way you can understand your spouse except by genuinely listening to them.
- Many times listening is done more effectively through *asking questions*.
- Learn to *distinguish between* the expression of feelings and the communication of facts. (Each requires a different response)
- Once your spouse feels that they have been *heard*, there is much less defensiveness and conflict to wade through.
- Good listening leads to *understanding*.

Understanding

Look back at the definition of communication. Notice that the result we are looking for in any act of communication is understanding. You could say that it is the goal of communication. Think about it... we talk to someone with the hope, and many times the expectation, that they will understand our words – thereby understand *us*!

Points to Consider

- Understanding only comes when you have a *genuine interest* in what is on your spouse's mind and heart. Don't expect to understand if you are eager to be done with the conversation so that you can get on to other things! And don't expect your spouse to be happy about it if that is your attitude!
- Because of the variety of things we may be responsible for in a given day, it is essential that we *prepare ourselves* to seek understanding when we know we are soon going to be with our spouse. Adjust your mindset as you are on the way!
- Understanding must be *verbally expressed* in the end. Your spouse needs to hear you say what you've understood, so that they can be assured that you "got it." They may also need to know what you think or feel about what they have said.
- If the understanding you receive reveals that your spouse has been hurt by you, *address the hurt.* The hurt may have resulted from a misunderstanding or mistake, but the reason doesn't matter. You need to let your spouse know that you are sorry they were hurt and make apologies where needed. To know that you've hurt your spouse and not apologize for that hurt, communicates that you are not sorry that they were hurt!
- A helpful way to assure your spouse that you understand what they have said, is to finish the conversation with tender, *physical* moments of acceptance and affirmation. (Hugs, touches, holding hands, etc.) An apology or expression of understanding without physical touch is like a dessert without taste (very dissatisfying).

- All communication needs to end in *affirmation* – take the opportunity to express love for one another. – Consider *1 Thessalonians* 5:11
- If your spouse expressed any *fears* during your conversation, explore those fears gently and with compassion. This communicates concern and care. If their fears are about the way you think or feel about them, reassure them of the truth of how you feel.

Finally, it may be helpful to you to think of understanding in some more colorful terms.

- Understanding is the peace at the end of a conflict...
- Understanding is the calm after a storm...
- Understanding is a warm, secure hug in the presence of fear...
- Understanding is reassurance in the face of doubt...
- Understanding is like rest after a long day of labor...
- Understanding is comfort for a misunderstood soul...
- Understanding is a cup of cool water to one who is parched and dry...

Questions for Reflection

- How do you feel when you are with a person who you know is not really listening to you? How often do you think others may feel that way about you?

- Set aside some time to ask your spouse how well you listen to them... and instead of being defensive, allow the Spirit to teach you, through them, to become a better listener.

- Oftentimes, questions are the key to good listening. For practice, consider the sentence below. Imagine that your spouse said it to you during a conversation. Write down as many questions as you can that would help you to explore what your spouse might be feeling.

  "*I'm feeling very discouraged about myself...*"

- Explain why understanding is so important to communication?

- Set aside some time to talk with your spouse about this issue of understanding. Ask your spouse how well he/she feels you truly understand them. Ask if they can think of any ways that you could improve in your efforts to better understand and know them.

SECTION FOUR:
Communication is Key

DAY 19

A Prayer Suggestion: Thank the Lord for the relevance of His word and the wisdom that it gives. Set your mind to truly hear and understand what God has to say to you today. Ask Him to lead you to greater understanding...

As we are learning, communication is one of the hubs around which the wheel of a healthy marriage turns. So much revolves around this one skill – and the good news is that everyone can learn to be better at honest communication! Let's look once more at our definition of healthy communication:

Definition: Communication is a *process* (verbal and non-verbal) of sharing information (thoughts, opinions, emotions, etc.) that includes *talking* and *listening*, resulting in *understanding*.

In today's lesson, we are going to consider 5 different levels on which communication happens, and consider the importance of those levels for a marriage relationship.

Five levels of communication

Level 1 – Cliché / surface communication

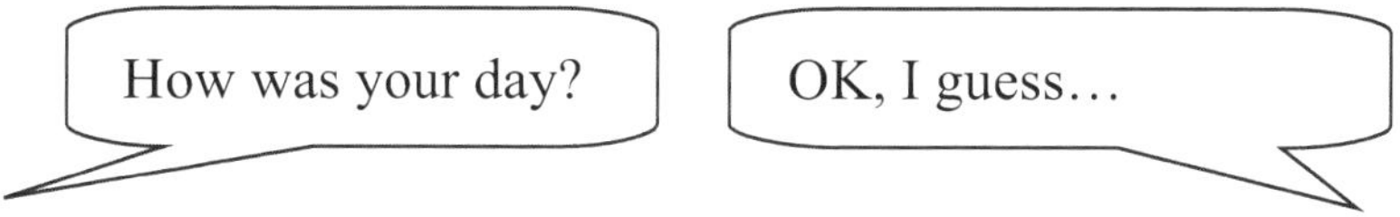

All of us speak on this level… with almost everyone we meet! It's the "Hi, how are you doing?" and the "Good… how are you?" that begins most conversations. While those questions could be very genuine and lead to some very meaningful and caring conversations, they typically don't. They are the "starter" phrases that most of us have learned to say in order to be polite.

What we want to notice about this level of communication is that it exists… and is necessary. It would be inappropriate and awkward if we shared everything with everyone right from the start of a conversation! I'm sure you've probably known people who do exactly that – and they are likely not the people you put first on your list of people to be with!

But let's consider this level of communication in light of the marriage relationship. Is there any place for this kind of "light" conversation in a marriage? Of course, there is a place for it in marriage – but no marriage can survive if this is the deepest the conversation ever goes. Marriage is to be a complete unity of a man and woman, and that kind of unity will not happen with "Level 1" conversations being the main, or only form of communication.

<u>Level 2</u> – Factual

"Level 2" conversations can be characterized as, "Just the facts Ma'am!" This is where we pass along information about people, schedules, routines, responsibilities, and other important things that are necessary or fun parts of our lives. Every couple interacts on this level, at least some of the time.

But sadly, some couples are very poor at this kind of communication, and feel the repercussions of it almost daily. Neglecting this type of communication causes wires to get crossed, family schedules to get confused, and frustration to quickly follow!

This kind of communication happens, not just out of need, but also out of consideration. If each marriage partner has not learned to be considerate of their partner, these kinds of details may seem unimportant or trivial. But the fact is, a family or a household cannot function smoothly if these things are not communicated regularly and considerately. In order to be healthy, your marriage *needs* this kind of communication almost daily.

Level 3 – Ideas & Judgments

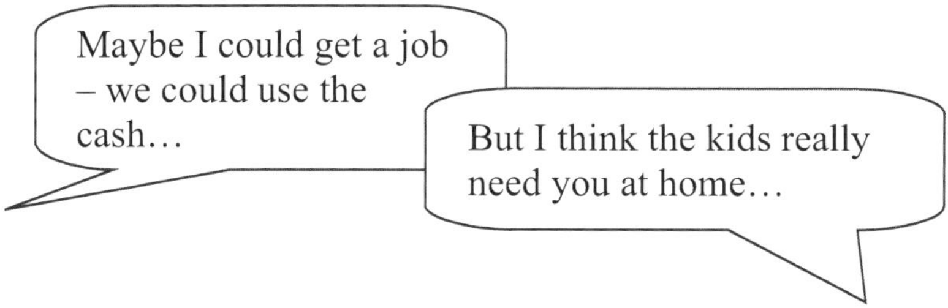

As you can see, each level of communication is moving deeper, to more substantial and important things having to do with your life together. "Level 3" communication is where each of you "risks" a bit more by revealing what you really think about certain subjects. This is often where conflicts arise, simply because the two of you are individuals, with differing ideas and thoughts.

It's important that every couple learns to share on this level, and to do so with grace and love for the other. Differing opinions should be discussed, understood, and worked out together, and may take a good deal of time to get through. But the important thing is that both of you are striving toward true unity. This doesn't mean that either of you should compromise on issues of right and wrong, but that you work together to discover what the Lord says about such things and come to a place of unity around His word.

Level 4 – Feelings & emotions

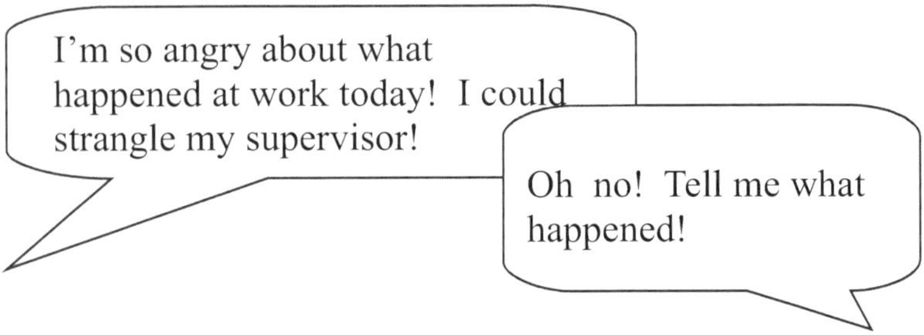

For many people, this level of communication is where they feel a bit "over their heads" and simply withdraw. The emotional level of expression can be quite intimidating, especially if you didn't grow up in a home where emotion was expressed very often.

A helpful thing to realize is that emotions are very seldom the last word. Instead they are indicators – barometers of deeper things that are going on in a person's heart or mind. Learning to understand and wade through the emotions of your spouse will go a long way in helping you to know them more deeply.

But that's only one side of the issue. There's also the need to be able to freely share your own emotions. For many people that feels too vulnerable, too risky, and they'd rather keep it all inside. But you have to understand, healthy marriage relationships *need* that level of deep sharing and communication. It's part of what makes two people become one as scripture teaches.

You may have a hard time even knowing what you feel, much less expressing it. But you shouldn't give up! Keep trying, and give it some time. If it's your spouse that has difficulty sharing his/her emotions, be patient, ask good questions, and wait for their response. The rewards could be tremendous!

Level 5 – Open & truthful

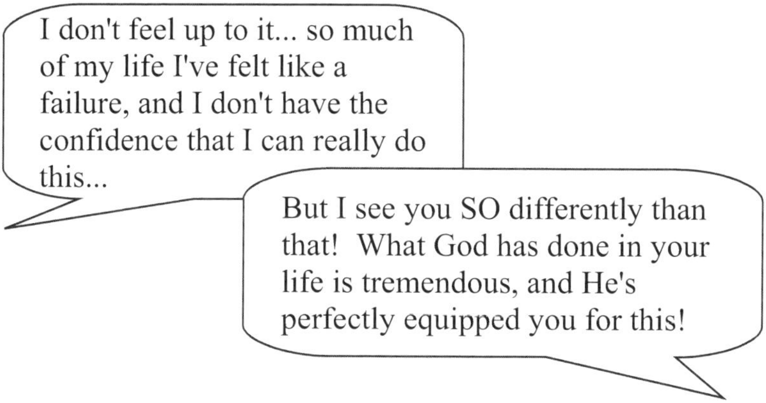

Couples who work hard to move their communication to "Level 5" are those whose marriages are full of security and joy in spite of the difficulties they face and the differences they may have with each other from time to time. The reason? They have learned to truly know each other, and to love each other deeply!

At this level of communication a husband or wife reveals personal doubts and insecurities, fears and dreams - hoping for the support and help that God wishes to give through their spouse. It's on this level that some of the most meaningful and transformative things take place!

But it can also be the level where some of the worst offenses are committed. You must learn to handle your spouse's total honesty with care, true concern, and with the love of Christ. It is that kind of love that begins to bring healing to the hurts that are shared, and victory to the struggles they face!

Questions for Reflection

- Take a few moments to talk together and pinpoint the levels of communication that the two of you engage in the majority of the time.

- Share with each other which levels of communication you personally find the most difficult.

- Take turns expressing your desires for your communication. Make sure that each of you expresses what kind of "responder" you want to be to your spouse at each level.

- Are there any of these levels of communication that you are "stuck" in, in a bad way?

DAY 20

A Prayer Suggestion: Today's lesson will focus on the difficulties that are involved in communication. Ask the Lord to reveal to you what difficulties are most common for you and for your spouse. Trust Him to lead you in dealing well with those things.

Once again, before we begin with new information, let's review the definition of good communication:

Definition: Communication is a *process* (verbal and non-verbal) of sharing information (thoughts, opinions, emotions, etc.) that includes *talking* and *listening*, resulting in *understanding*.

Today, we are going to consider some of the reasons communication can be so difficult, as well as look at some of the most common roadblocks to good communication.

Why Communication Can Be So Difficult

It's almost certain that you've experienced attempts at communication that were confused and convoluted. But you may not have taken the time to consider exactly what happened to cause such a mess! There are at least 5 different things that can occur in any attempt at communication... and it is helpful to be aware of what they are...

Anytime you try to communicate, there is...

- *What you mean to say.* Every person who opens their mouth to speak has something in mind that they want to communicate. They *intend* to say something specific.

- *What you actually say.* Depending on many factors, what actually comes out of your mouth may or may not be a true representation of what you really wanted to say!

- *What the other person hears you say.* Even in a situation where you say exactly what you mean to say, that's not the end of the story. The person who is listening very naturally and innocently filters what you say through their own background, view of the world, beliefs about life, emotional perspective, understanding of the scenario they are in, definition of words, experience with you, and thousands of other things! It's very common for the person who is listening to *hear* something different than what you intended or said!

- *What the other person says about what you said.* Depending on what they have understood, the person who is hearing you speak may respond in any number of ways. They may show you by their response that they got exactly what you meant...or they may say something that has nothing to do with what you said! In that case, for some reason, the communication has been blocked! Getting to the bottom of it can take time, and a lot of work!

- *What you think the other person said about what you said.* It is possible and happens quite often, that you mishear or misunderstand what the other person is saying in response to what you said! You may *think* they didn't get what you said, when they really did!

Can you see why good communication is so difficult? It not only involves the actual words that are said, but the true meanings of those words, the interpretation of those words, the application of those words, and many other things!

Communication Road-Blocks

There are many things that can block effective communication. The more you are aware of them, the more you'll be able to watch for them and avoid them! Let's consider a few that are the most common.

Ignorance – this can come in two forms

1. You simply don't know how to communicate. Either you were not taught how to communicate well as you grew up, or you have lost the ability for some reason (an accident, trauma, etc.)
2. But ignorance can also exist on another level. If you don't know the meaning of words or phrases that are being said to you, it can be very difficult to communicate in response.

What to do...

- First, *admit* the difficulty you have (to yourself and your spouse).
- If your spouse is better at communicating, *humbly allow* them to coach you along...
- Get *help* from outside sources (Christian books, people you respect, etc.)
- Don't *ignore* the problem...doing so will only make your

task harder and more prolonged.

- Walk in faith, based on God's truth about you, in spite of how you feel!

Fear

You may have fears in regard to communication that stem from any of a number of sources. You may...

- Fear rejection (If they know what I really think or feel they might reject me...)
- Fear hostility (If I share what I think or feel, they might get angry at me...)
- Fear conflict (I hate conflict. It's more peaceful to avoid talking about what I think...)
- Fear tension (If I share what I think and we disagree, then we're not going to have much peace in the home...)
- Many other things...

<u>What to do...</u>

- Take the time to *identify* exactly what you are afraid of. (Your spouse might have some ideas...)
- *Invite* the Lord to teach you where the fear comes from.
- Seek the *solution/healing* you need in biblical ways.
- Get *godly help* as you need it (don't be embarrassed – that is Satan's trick)
- *Pray* about the issue with your spouse continually. Your prayers will have a great effect in uniting you and bringing God's help to your situation.
- Walk in faith, based on God's truth about you, in spite of how you feel!

Hopelessness

- Depending on your track record in attempting good communication, you may have come to the conclusion that it won't do any good, so why bother.
- The reality is that good communication is one of the keys to a healthy and strong marriage – and God Himself wants you to have a strong, healthy marriage. So there's no reason to give up!

<u>What to do...</u>

- Pinpoint any *lies* you may be believing that are keeping you hopeless.
- Ask the Lord to *enable you* to address this problem with your spouse. If it is a situation where you see hopelessness in your spouse, biblical confrontation might be needed.
- Get *godly help* as you need it (don't be embarrassed – that is Satan's trick)
- Walk in faith, based on God's truth about you, in spite of how you feel!

Insecurity

- Again, depending on what you've experienced in life, you may have learned to believe things about yourself that is not true. Sometimes you may think...
    - I don't have anything worthwhile to offer...
    - I'm terrible at communicating...
    - He/she can get along fine without my input...
- Lies like this are damaging because they keep us from walking in faith, living according to what God says *He* desires to do in our lives.

What to do...

- *Invite* the Lord to teach you where the insecurity comes from.
- Pinpoint any *lies* you may be believing.
- Seek the *solution/healing* you need in biblical ways.
- Ask the Lord to *help you* address your discoveries with your spouse.
- Get *godly help* as you need it (don't be embarrassed – that is Satan's trick)
- Walk in faith, based on God's truth about you, in spite of how you feel!

Pride

- This too can manifest itself in several ways...
  - I don't need her / his input...
  - I'm just going to do what I think is best...
  - I can't admit that I have difficulty in this... what would he/she think of me?

What to do...

- Remember what *God says* about your marriage... you are to be one!
- Realize that you cannot do *anything* on your own. (John 15:5) You need Jesus' help every step of the way.
- Don't forget that your spouse is God's gift to you, to help you in these kinds of things. When you reject or avoid their help, you are avoiding one of the primary means through which *God* wants to help you!

Questions for Reflection

- Write down what is the most difficult or frustrating part of communication to you. Use the 5 points at the beginning of this lesson as a starting place if that is helpful.

- Examine your own difficulties with communication. Do any of the road-blocks mentioned describe you? Be honest with yourself and with the Lord...

- Set aside time to discuss your answer to the previous question with your spouse. Do your best to be honest about your struggle. Be sure to respond compassionately to the struggles your spouse may share.

- After hearing your spouse share their difficulties, do you part to assure them of your patience and willingness to work through it together. Let them know that you understand and desire to be a help to them, not a hindrance...

5

SECTION FIVE

Attacking Anger

SECTION FIVE:
Attacking Anger

DAY 21

<u>A Prayer Suggestion</u>: As you can see from the title of this section, you will be considering the very real temptation each of us has to be angry in inappropriate ways. Today ask the Lord to show you how He sees you in this area.

Divorce has become a very commonplace thing in our society. Most every family has been touched by the break-up of loved ones, friends, or co-workers. Consider the following question:

Q: How does a couple go from...

Standing before a preacher,
tender and starry-eyed,
making vows of eternal
commitment to each other…

Standing before a judge,
vindictive and mean,
intentionally hurting and
attacking each other…

A: They got there one drop of unresolved anger at a time.

Facts about anger

- *Anger is a natural and normal part of life.*
  There is nothing in the scriptures that even imply that anger is "wrong." Anger is typically a reactionary or secondary emotion. It flows out of disappointment, hurt, misunderstanding, helplessness, or any of a

hundred other things. You need to understand that angry tendencies in you or in your spouse, are very natural and normal.

- *You will never be so spiritual or mature that you won't get angry.*
  If you read the scriptures very carefully, you can find situations where even Jesus was angry. Anger is part of life. You need to become comfortable with that fact.

- *The important thing about anger is how you deal with it.*
  Even Jesus got angry, but what He did with His anger is of the utmost importance! There was never a time when Jesus' anger moved Him to sin. We can be encouraged that just as we are tempted toward inappropriate expressions of our anger, Jesus was too.

- *You will either learn to deal with your anger, or your anger will deal with you.*
  You know people who you consider to be an "angry person." Their anger has consumed them, and you don't like to be around them. They are like an active volcano that you expect could go off at any moment. In order to live a healthy, strong, and purposeful Christian life, you need to deal with any anger problems you might have. If you don't, your anger will run *and* ruin your life.

Anger is like gunpowder in a bullet shell – you can pack it down, day after day after day. But if it is not adequately dealt with, the day will come when something *will* spark it!

God's Antidote to Anger

As you might expect, God has a great deal to say about anger. Let's look at a few passages:

> ***Ephesians 4:26-27*** – *Be angry and do not sin; do not let the sun go down on your anger, and give no opportunity to the devil.*

Notice that there are a number of "parts" to what these verses tell us about rightly handling anger...

- ***Be angry***... as mentioned before, anger is a very natural response. And in some instances it is a right response to a sin or injustice that has occurred.
- ***Do not sin***... Our responsibility in the matter is to keep a tight reign on our anger, not allowing it to drive us into sinful attitudes or behaviors.
- ***Do not let the sun go down***... The point here is that anger must be dealt with in short order. You are not to harbor it, nursing along a grudge, nor are you to ignore it or pretend it doesn't exist. You *must* learn to deal with your anger sooner rather than later.
- ***Give no opportunity to the devil***... When you refuse to healthily deal with your anger about any issue, the devil has an open door into your life. He will slip in and begin to do what he does best... stir up trouble!

> ***James 1:19-20*** – *Know this, my beloved brothers: let every person be quick to hear, slow to speak, slow to anger; for the anger of man does not produce the righteousness of God.*

Again, notice the various parts of this passage...

- ***Be slow to anger***... You have to learn, with the help of the Holy Spirit, to control your temper so that you are able to remain calm in the face of upsetting news or hurtful or frustrating circumstances. This is an outgrowth of your faith that God has all things under control.
- ***Your anger doesn't bring about God's righteousness*** – Human anger, the type of anger that produces vengeful attitudes and bitter feelings, does absolutely nothing to bring about the righteousness God desires for the situation.

As you begin today's "Questions for Reflection" ask the Lord to give you His mind about your anger...

Questions for Reflection

Spend a few moments in personal evaluation as you consider the following questions...

- Would other people consider me an "angry" person? (the following are warning signs)
  - Do I lash out at others?
  - Do I quickly become upset about things I don't like?
  - Do I respond defensively or harshly?

- When do I express anger toward my spouse?
  - When he/she has hurt me?
  - When he/she has disappointed me or let me down?
  - When he/she isn't living up to my expectations?

- After pondering these things, how would you describe your "anger issues?"

- What would you say the Lord desires to happen with your anger?

- Do you see that you are responsible to make that happen?

DAY 22

<u>*A Prayer Suggestion*</u>*:* Ask the Lord to prepare you for what He has to reveal in today's lesson. Renew your commitment to working through difficult issues for the health and strengthening of your marriage.

As we saw in the last session, anger is a very real part of every human relationship. It is normal and natural – but that is not an excuse for the wrong expression of anger. Every Christian is responsible to control themselves (with the Spirit's help) so that they do not sin even in their anger.

Many people grew up in homes where anger was not handled well, and as a result they picked up the same habits of expressing their anger as those whom they lived with. It's not unusual for people in that situation to be unaware that their angry behavior as inappropriate, unhealthy, or wrong. It's just what they do!

In today's lesson, we will be considering some of the ways in which people often handle their anger wrongly – so that you can examine yourself to see if there are any bad anger habits you have fallen prey to...

Anger handled wrongly

Threats

Threats are manipulation – plain and simple. It's the way many angry people have learned to get what they want. It's really a form of bullying. When you become angry with your spouse and begin to make threats (of divorce, withholding sex, harming them in some way, etc.) you are sinning with your anger.

Vindictiveness

Vindictiveness means that you do things to "get back" at the other person. It could be as simple as leaving a mess that you know they will have to clean up, or a more spiteful action like accusing your spouse of abuse or other actions that are untrue. Instead of being vindictive, you should work on the *reason* you are angry, thereby addressing the real problem.

Cursing/verbal attacks

Many times harsh words are an immediate response when anger rises to the surface. It's easy and quick but also terribly damaging to spit out hurtful or obscene words at your spouse. Most hurtful are words that attack the person for things they cannot change or easily address (weight, physical features, intelligence, etc.). These kinds of angry expression fall far short of the encouraging words we are expected to use as brothers and sisters in Christ (Ephesians 4:29).

Violence

Aggressive, intimidating behavior (punching walls, throwing things, hitting people) is an obvious expression of anger that is far removed from the loving, nurturing relationship that husband and wife are to share. Though this kind of anger is typically expressed more by men, it is becoming more prevalent for women to resort to this kind of angry behavior. Aggression, intimidation, and violence will destroy your marriage relationship.

Avoidance

Some people don't know how to deal with their anger, so they just stuff it. They avoid the issue that brought up the anger. This kind of person can make it seem like they are not angry at all, smiling and acting calmly. But the truth is there is a volcano inside, churning and boiling. But it's not always so "passive" in it's expression; it can manifest itself in other ways...

- *The silent treatment* – where one partner refuses to talk to the other for days, weeks, and even months at a time, instead of dealing with the issues that caused them to be so resentful.
- *Passive/aggressive behavior* – that's fancy psychology talk for subtle jabs, words, and actions that intentionally hurt another person, but are not obvious enough to confront easily.
- *Walking out of the room* – some people get so upset that they will walk out of the room, even while the other person is in mid-sentence. They may or may not come back, and may or may not want to talk about the issue later.

Demeaning attitudes and words

Some people don't hide their anger. Oh, they don't throw things or hit people, but they let you know they are not happy with you by demeaning and criticizing you any chance they get. From the way they talk you may believe that you never do anything right.

Instead of talking about the issues that have occurred, this person resorts to tearing down the person with whom they are upset... which does nothing to solve the problem or the conflict.

These are not the only ways that people handle their anger wrongly, but they are some of the main ones. Do you see yourself in any of these descriptions? Do you see your spouse? Spend some time seeking the Lord's perspective on your own behavior as you consider the following questions...

Questions for Reflection:

- Slowly re-read the wrong ways people deal with anger. Pause after each one, and ask the Lord to reveal things to you. Wait to see if he brings any situations to mind. What seem to be the ways *you* most commonly express your anger wrongly?

- Discuss your findings with your spouse. A good way to go about it may be...
  - Point out the ways *you* have wrongly handled anger, even using examples from your experience together.
  - Ask them to give their opinion about whether you are seeing yourself rightly. (Be sure not to get angry with them when they honestly share)
  - Where it is appropriate, confess your sinful behavior against your spouse, and ask for their forgiveness.
  - Remember, the Lord will forgive you too when you confess to Him.

DAY 23

A Prayer Suggestion: Today you will have the opportunity to learn one healthy way to approach situations that make you angry. Again, ask the Lord to open your heart and illuminate your understanding as you learn today.

The last session may have been very depressing, or convicting, or heart-breaking – depending on the past experiences you've had. The point was not to beat anyone up, but to reveal wrong for the sake of turning a corner to make things right. *That* is where we are headed today.

Anger handled rightly

Remember, anger is a secondary emotion, one that arises as a result of hurt, frustration, fear, or something else. When we can understand that first, it helps us to hit the "pause" button when we feel anger rising and move in some positive directions before it takes over. The following 8 guidelines are very helpful in learning how to get a handle on anger before it gets a handle on you.

Imagine yourself in a situation where you are in the first stages of an argument with your spouse (the kind where you wind up being angry with each other). As the heat begins to rise, think what it might be like if you were able to pause long enough to walk through the following steps...

Evaluate the situation and your responses from God's perspective.

- Did anyone do "wrong" in God's eyes?
- Is it a situation where feelings were hurt, but nobody really intended it to go that way?
- Is the way you are responding selfish or considerate?

If you believe wrong has been done, confront it.

- Even though you are confronting wrong, don't let your anger get the best of you and ruin the opportunity for a positive turn in the conflict.
- When you confront the wrong that you see, do so by focusing on God's viewpoint (utilize the clear teaching of scripture that applies to the situation).
- You may need to make your own humble confession of wrong, if you are the one who has been wrong.

If you find yourself responding wrongly (selfishly, defensively, too angrily) then you should stop and immediately make that right.

- More anger and wrong behavior will only feed the flames of the conflict. The minute you become aware that *you* are making things worse, stop and make it right.

Be Humble

- Whether you are the one wronged or the one who has done wrong, your humility will be huge in helping to diffuse and calm the situation. It's very hard to remain angry at someone who willingly considers and admits the possibility of being wrong.

Show care for the other person

- It may sound very strange to encourage you to be considerate of the person you are arguing with, but this is a very important point to understand.
- Many arguments and disagreements would go an entirely different direction if even one of the people involved kept in mind that they are called by God to love the other person.

Communicate

- Much of the reason that arguments don't get anywhere is because true communication gets short-circuited.
- Review the section on communication and consider what problems occur when anger overwhelms a desire to communicate clearly.

Desire to hear the other person, even more than you desire to be heard.

- Again, the lesson on communication revealed the vital importance of seeking understanding – and you can't get there if you're primarily concerned about getting words out of your own mouth!
- When you take the time to understand your spouse's position, you'll find that what you have to say might take on a very different flavor altogether!

Work through the conflict in a timely manner.

- Do you recall Ephesians 4:26-27? There the Lord tells us, "*do not let the sun go down on your anger...*"

- He's telling us that we are to work hard at making sure that our anger is not allowed unnecessary time to fester.

None of these guidelines is a "magical cure" to the problems you face when disagreements or tension arise, but they can go a long way in helping you deal with the situation carefully, considerately, and lovingly... and in a way that can handle your anger before it handles you!

Questions for Reflection

- Think about what a "typical" disagreement looks like in your relationship with your spouse. On a scale of 1 to 10 (1 = very little, 10 = very much), how much anger is typically involved or expressed?

- Which of the guidelines listed in today's lesson do you think would help you the most in those situations? Why?

- Set aside time to discuss the previous two questions with your spouse. Talk together about how you can work toward implementing the guidelines you both say would be helpful.

DAY 24

A Prayer Suggestion: Ask the Lord to remind you why you married your spouse in the first place. What were the things you saw in him or her that were appealing, that drew you to them? Keep those things in mind as you proceed today...

Marriage is a wonderful thing. God made it to be that way. But living in a fallen world we have a hard time always seeing it *as* a wonderful thing. There are times when the conflicts and adjustments needed in order for us to become "*one*" can seem unbearably difficult.

It's often in those difficult moments that we treat each other the worst. But that doesn't have to be the case if you will make a commitment to fight fairly.

What do I mean when I say, "fight fairly?" Take it back to elementary school when a fight broke out on the playground... and one of the brawlers hits the other with a low blow. The crowd of onlookers cries out in complaint. It's expected that certain things won't be done... and when they are, there's an outcry, at least somewhere deep inside.

In your marriage, you need to see your arguments the same way. There may be fights over various things from time to time, but in all of those instances you must learn to fight fairly.

Today's session has much to cover, and a great deal of new ground to explore....

Learning to Fight Fairly

Don't lose sight of the basics

Both of you must remind yourselves from time to time about the basics of what it means to be married. *The Marriage First Princple, the Cleaving Principle, the Unity Principle* – these and many other things are at the heart of a healthy marriage.

Over and above all of those is your calling to help each other become more like Christ. In the midst of an argument, these are the things that fly out the window! Fight for them now, when times are good, so that when times are difficult they will be more readily available to your mind.

Stop being defensive (it comes from pride or insecurity)

The truth is that all of us are imperfect. None of us gets everything right. Why then, do we get so defensive and angry when our spouse implies or says that we did something wrong? We should *expect* that we are going to miss the mark from time to time! It's simply how we are... and to be defensive is not only an obstacle to your communication, it's also stupid!

- Defensiveness stores up anger.
- Defensiveness blocks communication and intimacy.
- Defensiveness pushes your spouse away instead of drawing them close.
- Defensiveness goes contrary to *the Unity Principle* (oneness) – it makes you into adversaries, not partners.
- Dropping defensiveness means you have to learn to trust – each other, and more importantly, God.

Learn to express your viewpoint instead of accusing.

When the two of you get into a fight, work hard to honestly explain your preferences, your needs, and your feelings about the situation. It's important that your spouse hears what you think and feel.

But when you do so, be careful that you are not accusing your spouse. When you accuse, you are distorting the issue: it becomes:

- about their mistake.
- about their character.
- about their poor performance.
- an expression of your dissatisfaction with them

Accusing draws a conclusion about your spouse and condemns them for it. Attack the problem, not the person.

Give your partner permission to express themselves honestly, and vulnerably.

You need a "customer service counter" in your marriage, where each of you can come to express your dissatisfaction with things as they are, or how your needs are not being met. When you make room for this kind of interaction, the one receiving the criticism needs to have the attitude of:

- I'm here for you.
- How can I help?
- Your needs are my responsibility.
- I want to fix this together.
- I don't want you to feel that way, what can I do so that you won't?

That's what you vowed to do when you married, isn't it?

Begin with affirmation

- Use the sandwich approach – squeeze each expression of need between two affirmations.
- Read Proverbs 15:1-2, and Proverbs 25:11-12 together. Commit together to honoring the principles they teach as you discuss difficult matters.

Once dealt with, leave the past in the past.

- Dwelling on the past condemns your spouse to ongoing failure, which leads them toward discouragement and hopelessness.
- Dwelling on the past will destroy the future of your marriage.
- Take control of your thoughts by the power of the Spirit of God (2 Corinthians 10:5) and refuse to let your mind fixate on hurts or disappointments for which your spouse has asked forgiveness. If you've forgiven it, you need to leave it with the Lord.

Never allow yourselves to express anger sinfully.

- Two sessions earlier we covered this quite thoroughly. Review those ideas to make sure you understand them and know what you need to work on.
- Beyond that, you need to make a commitment between yourself, your spouse, and God that you will obey the admonition of Ephesians 4:29 in your interaction with each other. Being careful to say only what will build up the other person will go a long way in helping you avoid wrong anger.

Never allow anger to go underground.

- In the midst of a conflict, things are often said or implied that cause hurt. Naturally, anger may begin to show it's ugly head.
- When this happens, *deal with it right then*! Don't allow yourself to push it down inside to fester and grow. It is a cancer that will slowly kill the intimacy of your relationship.

Questions for Reflection

- Stop for a moment to consider the following words that are to be a part of marriage:
  - Unity
  - Partnership
  - Devotion
  - Love
  - Intimacy
  - Friendship
  - Companionship
  - Joy

- Write out your thoughts about these things as they exist now in your marriage relationship. How well do you and your spouse do at encouraging and facilitating them? Do you long for more of any of them? Write out what you'd like your marriage to be like in view of these things.

- Discuss your thoughts from the previous question with your spouse. Talk about the barriers that keep you from accomplishing your desires in these areas.

- Talk together about this question, "If you could keep these goals at the forefront of your minds when you begin to fight, how would your arguments be different?

DAY 25

A Prayer Suggestion: Ask the Lord to bring you to a place of godly resolve regarding the issue of anger in your marriage relationship. Ask Him to give you deep conviction that will lead to right action, that will lead to health in your marriage.

This week's study has been very full, of content and emotion! Today's lesson is going to be a time for you to process, and to pray, and to consider what God is saying to you about this issue of anger.

Read and meditate on the truths contained in the scriptures below. Take your time, depend on the Lord to reveal things to you, and listen to Him as He guides you toward change.

Write down anything that is helpful to you in understanding where you need to change, what you need to do in order to change, and how you can work with your spouse toward that change.

Scriptures to Consider

- *Proverbs 25:28*
- *Proverbs 29:11*
- *Proverbs 30:33*

Couple's Assignment

- Set aside time to discuss this issue together. Begin with prayer together, asking the Lord to open each of your eyes and to guide you to a healthier place.
- Looking back over your notes, discuss how each of you have typically dealt with anger in your relationship. (i.e. "I can see that I've been storing away anger and not really been dealing with things...")
- Talk together about how you can take steps to move away from those wrong ways of handling anger.
- Pray together, asking God to lead you in handling anger in the way HE desires you to.

SECTION SIX 6

The Husband's Role

DAY 26

A Prayer Suggestion: Spend some time in quiet listening, asking the Lord to prepare you for what He has for you to learn today and the rest of the week.

Each of us plays a variety of roles every day. Some are based on relationships, some are based on position, some are based on talents or skillls. Think about it: president, manager, brother, friend, guitarist, drummer, carpenter, engineer, mother, teacher – and the list could go on and on.

Roles are a very important and necessary part of the way groups and relationships are organized. Without them being clearly defined, we lack clarity and sometimes purpose.

Today's lesson will be a bit more heavy on the teaching side, because the groundwork for this week's topic needs to be laid very carefully and clearly. Today's we begin a week of consideration of the husband's role in the marriage relationship.

His role is not one based on his skills or his education. It's not a role that stems from his intelligence or his physical strength. It's a role that he's been appointed to, by God Himself, and is very much a step of faith requiring reliance on the Lord above all else.

The husband has been appointed by God to be the leader in the marriage relationship. Let's see this truth as it is described in the pages of scripture:

Ephesians 5:23 *For the husband is the head of the wife even as Christ is the head of the church, his body, and is himself its Savior.*

1 Corinthians 11:3 *But I want you to understand that the head of every man is Christ, the head of a wife is her husband, and the head of Christ is God.*

The way the word "*head*" is used in both of these passages is the same way we often use the word "*head*" in our culture. We speak of the "head coach" or the "head of the company." When we speak that way, we are speaking of a person who has been placed in a position of leadership or authority.

The first verse makes this clear by way of comparison... the husband is the head of the wife *even as Christ is the head of the church*. There's no question that Christ is the leader of the church – so we should have no trouble understanding what Paul is meaning here.

However, some argue, in a very complicated and misleading way that the Greek word for "head" (kephale), used in the original New Testament documents, means "source" and not "authority." The problem with this argument is that it simply isn't being honest with the facts.

Thus far in the study of ancient Greek literature, scholars have found 2,336 instances of the Greek word "kephale" being used in documents other than the scriptures. Out of those 2,336 uses of the word, only one of them convincingly means "source"- and in that instance it is speaking of the head or source of a river – *not* a human relationship.[3] In every other instance where the word "kephale" is used, and most clearly in those where human relationship *are* in view, it clearly means "authority."

In addition, *all* Greek Lexicons (Greek dictionaries) specializing in the type of Greek language spoken and written during the time of the New Testament, define the meaning of

3 Wayne Grudem, "Evangelical Feminism and Biblical Truth," Multnomah Publishers, Colorado Springs, 2004, p. 202

the word "kephale" as "authority."[4]

When Paul said that the husband was to be the "head" of the wife, it is a certainty that he meant to teach that the man is given a leadership role in the marriage relationship.

Why is this so important?

There are two reasons this issue is so important:

1. Cooperative relationships do not work well without clearly defined leadership. There has to be a structure or organization behind such relationships in order for them to function properly and healthily.
2. But more importantly, it is the way God arranged the marriage relationship to work! When God created male and female and placed them into relationship together, He did so in a way that would relate each of their unique natures to the other in a complementary way.

Many of the same people who wrongly insist that Paul did not mean "leader" when he said "head," will also insist that God did not originally create the relationship between Adam and Eve to function under male leadership. They say that such an idea is an outcome of sin. But is that true?

Look at Genesis 3 verses 6 & 9. In verse 6 we will see how sin came about and in verse 9 we'll see how God began to address the wrong that had been done...

> ***Genesis 3:6*** *So when the woman saw that the tree was good for food, and that it was a delight to the eyes, and that the tree was to be desired to make one wise, she took of its fruit and ate, and she also gave some to her husband who was with her, and he ate.*

4 Grudem, p. 206

Genesis 3:9 *But the LORD God called to the man and said to him, "Where are you?"*

In verse 6, we see that Eve was the first to sin. She was the one who was deceived by the serpent and brought sin into the world through her choice to eat the forbidden fruit. Only *after* sin had already occurred did Adam join her in it.

Yet, in verse 9, who does God go to in response to this sin? Was it Eve? No – it was Adam! God went first to the man, calling *him* to account for what had happened. This shows us that God had put Adam in the position of leadership in the relationship and held him primarily responsible.

We see this point reemphasized in the New Testament as Paul discusses the way sin came into the world:

1 Corinthians 15:21-22 *For as by a man came death, by a man has come also the resurrection of the dead. For as in Adam all die, so also in Christ shall all be made alive.*

Romans 5:12 *Therefore, just as sin came into the world through one man, and death through sin, and so death spread to all men because all sinned--*

In both of these contexts, Paul is speaking about how sin entered the world, and more importantly how the guilt of sin is removed through Christ! But don't miss that Paul refers to *Adam* as the one through whom sin came – *not* Eve. Why does he speak this way when Eve is clearly the one who sinned first? There can be no other explanation except that God sees Adam as the leader of the two – and therefore the one responsible.

Again, why is this so important? For two reasons:

1. Cooperative relationships do not work well without clearly defined leadership.

2. It is the way God arranged the marriage relationship to work!

While the first point is very true, and important in its own right, more important for your marriage on a practical level is the second reason... *God Himself* has created marriage to work best when His model for its organization and arrangement is followed. The Bible gives us instructions for how we are to relate to each other in human relationships – and the marriage relationship is no different.

Your marriage will work best, when you follow the model that God has intended for marriage. In the days to come we'll learn more about how this looks...and what it really means practically.

Questions for Reflection

- Take a quick assessment of your reaction to today's lesson. Overall, do you feel positively about what you've read, or do you feel negatively about what you've read?

- If you feel negatively, why is that? Do you have any *scriptural* basis for it? Could there be cultural influences or other things that are drawing you away from the idea of male-leadership in marriage? Ask God to show you.

- Sometimes negative feelings about male leadership in marriage come from instances of "male-leadership-gone-wrong" that you've experienced or seen in the past. Could it be that you are reacting to what you "think" male leadership looks like, and not what truly biblical male leadership is supposed to look like?

- Some men react negatively to the idea of male leadership in marriage simply because it makes them more accountable for their marriage than they would like to be. Examine your heart men. Is that anywhere in your motives? Ask God to show you.

- If you are still feeling negatively about this truth, do your best to reserve judgment about male leadership until you finish the week. You might be surprised at what male-leadership in marriage is – and what it is not.

DAY 27

A Prayer Suggestion: Do your best to be honest with the Lord about how you are feeling about this issue of male-leadership in marriage. Most importantly, ask Him to lead you to the place where you love what *He* loves in this area!

In today's lesson we will continue seeking to understand what the Bible means by male leadership in marriage. Interestingly, when it comes to commands or teachings about how to relate to your spouse, the Bible gives much more specific direction to men than it does women.

Today we will begin to take a look at some of those passages to see what they have to tell us about what a man's leadership in marriage should look like.

Sacrificial Love

Ephesians 5:25 Husbands, love your wives, as Christ loved the church and gave himself up for her...

The Apostle Paul was a master at illustration. His writings throughout the New Testament are filled with colorful examples to describe the truths that he taught. In this case, we find a very powerful illustration used to show husbands exactly *how* they are to love their wives.

The example he chooses to use is the example of Jesus. Just as Jesus willingly gave His life for the sake of those who would become His church, husbands are to willingly make the sacrifices needed to demonstrate their love for their wives.

It's important to realize that Jesus' love for His church caused Him to be extremely single-minded. Nothing could prevent Him doing what was needed to call people into His church – not governmental powers, and not His own execution. In fact, it was His death that made it *possible* for the church to exist at all. His desire for His "bride," the church, was one of the most consuming agendas of every day He lived.

Now transfer that idea to the role of a husband – the leader of his home. So many things press on husbands daily, screaming for attention. Work, children, responsibilities around the house, extended family relationships, etc., etc., etc. With such legitimate and important responsibilities continually at hand, it's difficult to think about squeezing something else into the list of priorities.

But God Himself has called you husband, to place your wife at the top of your priority list. Her needs, and her well-being are to be your number *one* priority next to your own relationship with God. It's *the Marriage First Principle* phrased in a different way.

For many men, this will mean stepping onto a road down which they have never been. For starters, those men will need to learn how to *think* differently about life, in light of what God is revealing about their role as leader of the family. God gives your wife to you as a partner, as a joy to your heart, and to be *cared for* with all that you are!

That means you are to care for her more than your work. More than your hobbies. More than your other responsibilities. You are to love her *first* – whatever that might take! That's what Jesus did for His bride, the church – and it is what you are called to do for yours! *It's called sacrifice, and it's the stuff godly men are made of!*

In the next lesson we will explore in greater detail what Paul is communicating in this analogy.

Questions for Reflection

- Read Ephesians 5:24-25. Do you see how the marriage relationship is designed in such a way as to demonstrate the relationship between Jesus and His church? Think about it... *your* marriage could show the world something about Jesus' love for them... and His desire to have them become a part of His "bride." Jesus *wants* your marriage to do that, and to do it well. Think about Jesus... and write down what He *did* because of His love.

- Though this concept may seem very overwhelming for the husband, and possibly hopeless for the wife, spend some time thinking about this: Clearly, no man can live out love for his wife in such a selfless way unless God enables Him to do so. But at the same time, God commands men *to* do so. You have to understand that God never commands His people to do something without also providing them the means or strength to do it. Ponder that for a while, and write down your thoughts...

- One of the last lines of the lesson said, "*It's called sacrifice, and it's the stuff godly men are made of!*" Can you think of likely reasons behind God calling the *man* to be the primary one to sacrifice in this way instead of the woman?

DAY 28

<u>*A Prayer Suggestion*</u>*:* Think of all the ways that various people have made sacrifices in order to show you love – time together in the midst of a busy schedule...a special, costly gift...a timely card or note. Think of the ways you have sacrificed for the ones you love. Ask the Lord to teach you more about the nature of sacrificial love in today's lesson.

In the last lesson we examined Paul's teaching about how a man should love his wife. By using the example of Jesus' love for his church, Paul made it very clear that the fundamental component of the love a man should have for his wife, is self-sacrifice. Today we are going to explore the extended passage of Ephesians 5:25-30 to discover some of the ways that this type of love is to be carried out. First, let's look at the entire passage...

Ephesians 5:25-30 *Husbands, love your wives, as Christ loved the church and gave himself up for her, that he might sanctify her, having cleansed her by the washing of water with the word, so that he might present the church to himself in splendor, without spot or wrinkle or any such thing, that she might be holy and without blemish. In the same way husbands should love their wives as their own bodies. He who loves his wife loves himself. For no one ever hated his own flesh, but nourishes and cherishes it, just as Christ does the church, because we are members of his body.*

The most obvious thing, worthy of being repeated, is that this trait of self-sacrifice *is the overarching and defining mark of husbandly love.* A husband is to care for his wife first – even before his own needs, so that she experiences in a very real way, the love that he has for her (which will serve also as a reflection of the love Christ has for her).

But there are some specific characteristics of this self-sacrificing love that Paul identifies that will help to define it more clearly. We'll begin by looking again at verses 26 and 27... and see how they highlight the first of our points for today...

Always for her good

> *26 that he might sanctify her, having cleansed her by the washing of water with the word 27 so that he might present the church to himself in splendor, without spot or wrinkle or any such thing, that she might be holy and without blemish.*

Look carefully at the words that Paul uses to describe the *reasons* behind the love Jesus has for His church. The many loving sacrifices Jesus made were "*that he might sanctify her,*" to "*cleanse her,*" to present her "*without spot or wrinkle,*" "*that she might be holy and without blemish.*" Jesus' focus for the church was ,and still is completely *for her good*.

What Paul is pointing out is that Jesus loved the church, *His* bride (you and me) in such a way that we are better for it! That is a love worthy of our imitation – and Paul says that husbands are to do exactly that! When a man endeavors to love his wife as Christ loves His church, he is to love her intentionally, for her good. His love should have purpose, intention, and determination so that his wife is better off through having been loved by him.

And look again at the areas where Jesus places His attention in loving His church... they primarily have to do with the personal, spiritual growth of the church. Jesus' desire for His church is not primarily what she does or accomplishes in the world (though powerful results of this kind will naturally follow). Jesus is more concerned with the character of the church, the inner qualities of holiness and righteousness that best represent His desires for her. In short, Jesus is more concerned with who His bride *is*.

Husbands need to pay heed to this observation. Your goal is to love your wife in such a way that you are helping her to grow in spiritual and personal maturity. This in *no way* implies that she is incapable or unfit to attend to these things for herself...but rather that these vital areas are where a husband's love is to most benefit his wife, because they are at the core of who the Lord Jesus desires her to be. This idea leads to the next point...

In a nourishing way

Looking again at verse 29, we see that part of what is to be in a husband's mind as he is intentionally loving his wife is that he be doing so in a way that nourishes her. Nourishment is a word we primarily use in the context of nutrition and diet. The foods we eat fuel our bodies for daily activity and ongoing health, which enables us to move ahead in life in a way that honors God.

A husband's self-sacrificing love for his wife is intended by God to serve her in a similar way. The spiritual, emotional, physical, and intellectual needs she has as a woman are to be his concern. His love is to provide her the security, assurance, affirmation, and strength that God *only* gives through the unique relationship she has with her husband.

In a cherishing way

When Paul says that a husband is to "*cherish*" his wife (vs. 29), he's saying a great deal. The word communicates first of all, that the husband is to see his wife as a person of great value and importance. She is to be held very high in his esteem. He is to see her as a treasure with which he has been entrusted. She is his partner to be honored and respected.

It is from these foundational attitudes about her that his intentional and tender care for her flows. We're talking about more than simple good intentions. A husband needs to take action in order to love his wife in this cherishing way. This consists of regular, caring connection with his wife, for the sake of caring for her.

This care may be manifested through such things as checking in with her regularly, asking questions about her life, taking the pulse of her feelings and thoughts regularly, and praying with her regarding those and other things. A man who learns to cherish his wife, as Christ does His church, will be one of the Lord's greatest blessings to her, and will be used greatly by God in her life.

A benefit to him as well

Look at verses 28-30 again...

> *28 In the same way husbands should love their wives as their own bodies. He who loves his wife loves himself. 29 For no one ever hated his own flesh, but nourishes and cherishes it, just as Christ does the church, 30 because we are members of his body.*

While it is not his primary motive, a husband's self-sacrificing love for his wife blesses him in the end. This is a wonderful, and very clear example of how God's commands to His people carry their own blessings. We can see this to be true if we follow his actions to their logical conclusion.

As he loves his wife with Christ-like, self-sacrificial love, she is blessed, benefited, and grows in her spiritual capacity for maturity and faith. As those qualities become greater in her, she is able to live out that maturity in the family, benefiting her children, husband, and home. God has created a beautiful cycle of health and blessing in our marriages that begins when we walk in obedience to His instructions for us.

Questions for Reflection

Today's questions are intended primarily for the husband, as a tool for self-evaluation. Take whatever time you can throughout the week to answer these questions carefully...

- Give your thoughts about the following statement from today's lesson: *"...this trait of self-sacrifice is the overarching and defining mark of husbandly love."*

- Go back and read the first paragraph of the section called *"In a cherishing way."* Do you see your wife in the ways described? Write down why you think you do or do not see her in this light. This is where self-sacrificial love begins. If you don't value your wife as God intends, you will find it very hard to love her as you should.

- Spend some time thinking about what it might mean for you to better nourish your wife. Can you think of some practical things (they don't have to be huge things) that you can begin doing right away to begin nourishing her more? Consider the areas mentioned: spiritual, emotional, physical, intellectual.

- Describe in your own words what point was being made in the final section of today's lesson. Do you see that God wants to use your obedience to His commands to bring blessing to your own life?

SECTION SIX:
The Husband's Role

DAY 29

<u>*A Prayer Suggestion*</u>*:* Continue to ask the Lord to open your heart to what He desires your marriage to look like. Ask Him to enable you to see it more clearly today.

In the last two lessons we explored the way marriage was created to be – and learned that part of that has to do with the role of leadership the husband is to carry out. Remember, no man is the leader of his home because he deserves it, or because he's smarter or better than his wife. He's the leader simply because God has appointed him to be the leader.

It's a role of humble responsibility. The last lesson also began uncovering more of the details of what a husband's leadership should be like. At the heart of it is a self-sacrificing love for his wife – a love that reflects the kind of love Jesus has for His church.

In attempting to understand this type of love the scriptures give us a great deal of help. There are three primary principles about a husband's love for his wife that we can glean from other passages of scripture. We'll address two of them in this lesson, and one in the next. The first two come from the same passage of scripture...

> ***1 Peter 3:7*** *Likewise, husbands, live with your wives in an understanding way, showing honor to the woman as the weaker vessel, since they are heirs with you of the grace of life, so that your prayers may not be hindered.*

Live with her in an understanding way

The first thing a husband is instructed to do in loving his wife sacrificially is to *live with her in an understanding way*. Literally, the Greek says for him to live with her "*according to knowledge*." In order to do this, a man needs to be a student of his wife, getting to *know* how God has knit her together as a person.

He needs to understand how she thinks, what is important to her, what is hurtful, and what is encouraging. He needs to work at discovering what gives her joy and what builds her faith. The more he knows these things the more able he is to love her effectively in the circumstances they will face together. And in learning these things, he's actually showing her love!

Living with her "according to knowledge" also means that he needs to understand her uniqueness *as a woman*. It may seem too obvious to say, but she is *not* a man. She doesn't view things like a man does. She doesn't behave like a man, handle life like a man, or approach things like a man. She is a woman – and God made her to be a woman!

Husbands, Peter wants you to realize that your wife is *entirely* different from you in the way she is made. She is a woman... a beautiful and wonderful creation of God, designed by Him for His good purposes. Instead of resisting or resenting the differences between you and your wife, learn to appreciate them, respect them, and *understand* them.

Seek to know why God created her so differently than you. Seek to understand how much God intends for the two of you to complement each other. A husband who is going to love his wife as he should needs to understand and value the things about his wife that are different from him.

Show honor to her

Next, Peter says a husband is to *show honor to his wife*. What does that mean – to show honor to her? All kinds of images might come to mind... but most helpful might be a simple definition. To honor someone is to show them "high respect." When a husband shows honor to his wife, he will highly respect her, as a person and as a partner in their marriage relationship.

Too often, and for a variety of reasons, husbands merely tolerate the way their wife is, enduring the differences instead of treasuring them. He may begin to resent her instead of honoring her. Peter is wanting every Christian husband to see that part of the way you love your wife well is to treat her well...as a person of value. Listen to her when she speaks. Value what she has to say. Take time to understand her heart. Treat her as a valuable treasure – because she is!

He gives two reasons why a husband is to show his wife honor. 1) because she is the "*weaker vessel.*" and 2) because she is an heir of the grace of life found in Christ, right alongside her husband. Let's take these one at a time to get a clear picture of what they mean...

A word picture that has proven extremely helpful to many in understanding exactly what Peter is trying to communicate here, is to think of the husband as a plastic storage container and the wife as fine crystal.

A plastic storage container is made in such a way as to withstand a certain amount of abuse. It's made to be durable and sturdy. It's microwavable and dish-washer safe. In short, it's tough.

But fine crystal on the other hand, can't be treated in such rough ways or it will break. Instead, it is to be handled with care, concern, and value – in short, it is to be honored (highly respected).

When Peter says that the wife is the "*weaker vessel*" he's in no way implying that women are incapable, inferior, or weak in terms of their character. He's also not suggesting that husbands should be patronizing or condescending toward their wives. What he is telling husbands is that you need to understand that in some very basic ways, your wife is very, very, *VERY* different from you.

You can take the bumps and bruises of life, the backhanded comments of disrespectful or rude people. And you can handle the difficulties that come your way with a toughness that is unique to men.

In contrast, your wife will tend to take things much more personally and be wounded much more deeply by the things that happen to her. She's more delicate, like the crystal. That means she can easily be damaged by the way that *you* treat her as well.

The second reason Peter gives as to why husbands should honor their wives is that as a fellow Christian with you, your wife will one day receive the fullness of life in Christ that you will. On that glorious day when Jesus returns, both of you will stand before him as equal heirs of the grace of life that Jesus died to provide for His church.

This reminder is very needed, because many men have taken their appointment to a position of leadership in the home to mean something it doesn't. They have come to think more highly of themselves than they do of their wives.

Domineering attitudes, dictatorial rule, and physical and emotional abuse can all stem from this wrong-headed notion that leadership means superiority. Husbands, your wife is a *co-heir with you* – and God is the one who has made it so. Treat her with honor, because God has honored her with life in Christ just as He has you.

In our next session, we'll explore another practical way that husbands are to love their wives.

Questions for Reflection:

Today's questions are designed to help the two of you become aware of areas of need in your relationship. Remind yourselves right now that you are doing this study to learn, to grow, and to make your marriage stronger. Any way that you are able to learn an area of weakness or failing, and make some course corrections, is a blessing to both of you. Fight the temptation to become defensive.

- This one is for both husband and wife to answer. On a scale of 1 to 10 (1 = poor, 10 = tremendous), how would you rate the husband in your relationship on how well he "*understands*" the wife, in all her uniqueness as a woman?

- On that same 1 to 10 scale, how would you rate the husband on how well he *lives with* the wife in an understanding way? In other words, how well does he practically "life out" the knowledge that he has?

- Compare your answers. Take turns explaining why each of you made the ratings you did. Talk about how the husband might improve both his understanding of his wife, and his application of that knowledge. Husbands, keep in mind that your wife's opinion on this weighs very heavily... since she's the one who needs to feel understood!

DAY 30

A Prayer Suggestion: Ask God to clearly show you, what kind of husband Jesus would have been if He had married. Take your time. Consider how He would have expressed care, honor, respect, and love for His wife. Ask the Lord to begin the miracle of reproducing Himself in the husband in *your* marriage.

Today's lesson wraps up our week-long focus on the role of the husband in marriage. We've seen that he's to be the leader in the relationship, but we've also seen that his leadership is *never* to be domineering or overbearing. It is a leadership built on self-sacrificing love.

That is the kind of love Jesus has for us, His bride, and it is the kind of love every husband is to have for *his* bride too! Can you picture Jesus being domineering or overbearing toward His bride? In today's lesson, we will examine one of Paul's instructions about a husband's love for his wife...

No harshness

Colossians 3:19 *Husbands, love your wives, and do not be harsh with them.*

The two main words in that sentence, "*love*" and "*harsh*" don't even seem to belong in the same sentence, do they? Paul's straightforward way of stating it helps us to see that they *don't* belong together in any way. They are opposite currents, flowing out of completely different springs. Love flows from a self-sacrificing concern, care, and compassion for another person, while harshness flows out of a self-absorbed, self-centered desire.

If Paul wants husbands to make sure that they are not being harsh with their wives, it would be helpful to know exactly what the word means. Simply, harshness can be defined as behavior that is "grim or unpleasantly severe; stern and/or cruel."

Harshness flows out of a *lack* of concern for the individual with whom you are dealing. It does not consider their good, their feelings, or their perspective, but rather seeks to advance its own agenda regardless of what it might do to the other person. That is clearly an attitude and approach that is nothing like the Christ-like love we've been considering over this week.

Chances are that very few husbands reading this would say that they *want* to be harsh with their wives. It's even more certain that no wife reading this wants to be treated harshly! But let's be honest. Husbands can and often do resort to harshness, and many times don't even realize they are doing it! What sorts of things would push a husband who otherwise truly desires to love his wife, to treat her harshly?

Sometimes the tendency toward harshness comes from the fact that men and women are different. Here are some oft-repeated phrases heard throughout the course of my counseling experience that serve as good examples:

- "Why won't he ask for directions?"
- "Why does she always want to talk about the relationship?"
- "Why can't he see that something is bothering me?"
- "Why doesn't she understand that I'm tired when I get home?"
- "Why do men never remember and women never forget?"

Get the picture? Men and women simply operate differently...and it's very easy and quite common for the husband *or* the wife to be irritated by those differences. That irritation simmers under the surface and comes out in a variety of ways. When Paul tells husbands not to be harsh, he's saying two things:

1. "Husbands, be careful... this may be your tendency when you are frustrated or irritated." and
2. "Husbands, your wife can't handle your harshness -and shouldn't be expected to."

Husbands, can you see that a harsh response toward your wife is likely a response to something about her that you don't understand or don't appreciate? It's an irritation you feel that prompts you toward manhandling the situation... and your wife!

It's in those moments that we husbands do some of the most damaging things to our wives and don't even know it. The way she deals with things may be very different from you, but nevertheless you are responsible before God to learn to understand that part of her and learn not to be harsh toward her because of your own irritation or frustration.

Examples

Following are a few examples of differences between husband and wife that sometimes prompt a harsh response from the husband. Clearly, these are generalizations, so apply them to what is true of your relationship... But also be careful not to overlook something in the list that the Lord may be wanting to point out to you about yourself! Read them carefully and slowly, putting yourself in each situation...

- It's common for men to think their wife is "wrong" because she's not "logical" or thinking of things like he does. The truth is that she's not wrong, just different. Of course she has room for growth in regard to her emotions, but for you to disregard her opinions or thoughts simply because she expresses them emotionally is to turn toward harshness in how you deal with her.
- She is very concerned about the details of situations and relationships, while he may be much more casual about those things. Again, there is no right and wrong about this difference, and for a husband to become irritated by his wife's interest in the details of conversations or situations, is again turning toward a harsh response toward her.
- Like anyone else, husbands sometimes simply want to do their own thing. To come home to the pressing needs of his wife or kids can be an irritation when he is looking forward to a relaxing evening in his recliner. When he allows himself to respond harshly out of this irritation, there is nothing else to call it except "selfishness." A husband's job description has no schedule. In fact, his *true* job is at home! Don't allow yourself to be absorbed by your own desires, to the neglect and harm of your wife and family. Harshness will be a natural by-product if you do.
- This last example may be one of the more difficult ones to discern, so ask the Lord to guide you to see what is true about you. There are many men, Christian and non-Christian who, if the truth be told, really do look down on women. You can hear it in the comments they make, and see it in the way they treat them. If this is true of you, on any level, you will wind up treating your wife in a demeaning and sometimes harsh way – at

least at times. Let the Lord reveal to you whether this is true of you... and ask Him to make the needed changes in you to remove that destructive attitude once and for all!

Suggestions for growth

To finish up this week's topic, we will end with some suggestions for husbands about how to cultivate a right attitude about their wives that will help them to move away from harshness in their responses and behavior.

- Take time to evaluate the way you respond to your wife overall. Even ask her opinion about ways that you respond to her that she considers harsh.
- Don't disparage the things about your wife that are different from you. Guard yourself against looking upon those things with contempt or disdain.
- Work hard at learning what things about your wife *are* different than you, along with why she is that way.
- Learn to value the differences, because they exist by God's design!
- Remember, her viewpoints, her perceptions, her intuition, and her outlook on life and the world are no more perfect than yours, but *to disregard them because they are not yours is the height of pride, and a great foolishness that will bring disaster to your marriage!*

Finally, as an introduction to next week's lessons, remind yourself that God gave your wife to you as your helper because you need her help! It's the sovereign plan of our sovereign God that you work together in a complementary way for His glory and purpose!

Questions for Reflection

Today's questions are intended to help the husband evaluate how he is doing in his role.

- Harsh: "grim or unpleasantly severe; stern and/or cruel." While you may not see yourself as this type of person overall, think through ways that you might respond to your wife that could appear harsh to her. After writing down possibilities, ask her for her input about your list! Be ready for any additional situations she recalls...

- Write out your thoughts about the suggestion that harshness usually flows out of frustration or irritation you feel because of differences between the two of you.

- Do you see any things in the "examples" section that you can pinpoint as differences between you and your wife that have caused you to be harsh in the past? Are there any others you can think of that are not listed?

- Look over the "Suggestions for Growth." Are there any that stick out to you as particularly relevant to your situation?

- "Remember, her viewpoints, her perceptions, her intuition, and her outlook on life and the world are no less important than yours, but *to disregard them because they are not yours is the height of pride and a great foolishness that will bring disaster to your marriage!"* Write your thoughts about that statement.

7

SECTION SEVEN

The Wife's Role

DAY 31

<u>*A Prayer Suggestion:*</u> Begin by thanking the Lord for His provision of wisdom. Thank Him for the beauty of marriage. Ask Him to show you how you can better carry out your role in the marriage relationship so that your marriage can bring greater glory to Him.

As mentioned in the last section, there are many more specific instructions in regard to marriage responsibilities that are directed to the husband, than there are to the wife. Nevertheless, the wife has been given a role within the marriage that is vitally important, and there are both scriptural descriptions of her role and scriptural instructions for how to carry it out that are worth our attention.

As we've done before, we'll begin with a lesson that is heavy on content, due to the importance of establishing a good foundation upon which to build. Let's begin by returning to the book of Genesis. There we will find God's description of why He made Eve, the first wife...

We pick up the story after God has created the world, formed a man from the dust of the ground, and put the man in the garden to care for it. It is at that point that God says these remarkable words...

Genesis 2:18 *Then the LORD God said, "It is not good that the man should be alone; I will make him a helper fit for him."*

God makes no mistakes. Ever. Whatever He does, in whatever way He does it, is for a specific and good purpose.

Sometimes His purpose is readily apparent, other times it remains a mystery to us. There are still other times when, with thoughtful consideration and the revealing ministry of the Holy Spirit, we can come to understand the reasons behind God's actions. It is this third situation in which we find ourselves as we consider this verse.

There are some details about the situation described here that we need to consider. For example, God made the male human first, with no companion. In other words, for some time Adam was the only human on the planet! And God Himself pointed out that it was "*not good that the man should be alone.*"

Did God suddenly realize that He had made a mistake by making Adam all alone? Not at all! There was absolutely *no* mistake! God *intentionally* created Adam first and all alone - and for a good purpose! What was that good purpose? Look carefully at the words God uses and we will find the first of at least two purposes God had in making Adam alone initially.

First, He's wanted to make a statement about human nature. We need companionship! It's part of how He's wired us. God said, it is *not good* for us to be alone. We are social creatures, in part because we are created in the image of God (Genesis 1:27), who also exists in a social relationship within the Trinity.

This may seem a bit off subject, but it's very important for us as human beings to realize that we need each other. No man or woman can or should function all alone, whether they are married or not.

There is an interdependence that God has built into us that we are wise not to ignore. In marriage, that is particularly true. When a man and woman become husband and wife, they are entering into a relationship that God Himself established as a blessing, so that they could each have a complementary partner with which to share their lives.

If we were able to read this passage with no preconceived knowledge of where the story was going, we'd feel a sense of anticipation at this point in the account! What is God going to do? Our best guess might be that He's going to make another person...but not necessarily a female. All we know is that He's promised to make a "*helper fit for him.*"

Let's stop for a moment and closely examine the exact words the Lord used in describing who He was going to make to be Adam's companion. In the original Hebrew, the Lord says, "I will make a(n) 'ezer neged'." Those two words are tremendously important. The word "ezer" simply means "help" or "helper." The word "neged" means "counterpart" or "corresponding part." So we can see that God's intention was to make a "helper who corresponds to the man." And then, He created Eve.

It is essential to notice that the *only* word God uses in the creation account that describes Eve's role in the marriage relationship is "*helper.*" He does not call her "partner," though that is indeed a true description of the relationship a wife shares with her husband. God does not call her "friend," though every married couple should surely be the best of friends. God doesn't even refer to her as "companion," even though it is clear even in this context that she was created to be Adam's companion! The only word God Himself used to describe Eve's function and role was these two Hebrew words that mean "helper who corresponds to him."

Here is where we see the secondary purpose of God's solitary creation of the man. He created Adam alone initially not only to show that He *needed* a companion, but also to show that he was not equipped to carry out God's plans for humanity all on his own. He needed someone else to come alongside him, to help him, and to be his counterpart in displaying the image of God in the world... and that counterpart was his wife, Eve.

Something that is important to recognize is that the role a person plays has nothing to do with their identity or their value. For example, I fill many roles – husband, father, Pastor, friend, brother – but none of them is my identity, and none of them communicates my value. My identity is *who* I am, not what I do. My value flows out of being a human being, created in the image of God.

The same can be said of Eve... she was a human being, created in God's image, *co-equal* with Adam in terms of value and importance. Her identity was Eve, but her role in the marriage was helper. Without her, Adam would be unable to sufficiently carry out what God desired for him.

There is a difficulty many have at this point because our culture has taught us that equality has to apply across the board, in every area of life in order for it to be true equality. But that simply is not the truth. For example, every one of my 5 children is completely equal with me in terms of value, humanity, importance, and significance. But none of them is equal with me in terms of roles within the family. None of them should be or can be the Dad, even though they are my equals!

We can see the very same type of situation in the interrelationship that is shared among the members of the Trinity. Each of them is co-equal *as god* (all three are divine). But, they are *not* all Father, or Son, or Spirit. They each carry out different roles, but are all equal in their divinity. If we are not careful to make this distinction, our thinking can get very confused!

Just as we see in the relationship shared among the members of the Godhead, we can see that when Eve was made as Adam's "*helper*" – it in no way meant that she was less than him, or unequal to him. She was *completely and totally* equal with him (made in the image of God) – but each of them was assigned a different role in the relationship.

Questions for Reflection

- Think through the significance of Adam being created alone initially. Write out your thoughts about why God did it that way.

- Describe how the wife's role in marriage has nothing to do with her value, but rather is a role that's been assigned to her by God.

- In your own words define what "*helper*" means as it is related to the wife's role in the marriage relationship.

- For you personally, is the idea of the wife being a "*helpe*r" difficult to accept, or easy? Why do you think that is?

- Explain in your own words how a person can be equal in value and significance, but different in terms of the role they play. Write down some examples from everyday life of this kind of situation, if you can think of any.

DAY 32

<u>A Prayer Suggestion</u>: Spend a few moments being still before the Lord. Calm your mind and spirit. Push away every distraction that might keep you from hearing from Him today. Submit every burden, care, and anxiety to Him. If you are feeling any tension about the topics being discussed in this section of studies, remember that He only desires you to live in the truth. Ask Him to guide you to understand His truth as it is revealed in His word.

The last study introduced a topic that is very difficult for many people. There are a variety of reasons for this...

- Some were raised in a situation where the man of the house was domineering or abusive to the women in the family. It would be natural for that person to be leary about the topic being covered here.
- There are others who have believed a lie, preached by our culture, that there are no significant differences between women and men.
- Still others may have been raised in a church setting where the biblical concepts we are discussing in these lessons were used to oppress and stifle women in the name of Christ. That person is understandably cynical about this topic from the beginning. But the truth is that using the scriptures to those ends is inexcusable, and not at all what God intended.

No matter what your background, or why you may feel misgivings about this topic, I want to encourage you to press on. Don't throw out the beautiful, complementary ways the Lord has instructed us to function in marriage, because a person in your past misapplied these truths. What God has instructed for husbands and wives is a wonderful relational structure that leads only to His blessing.

In today's study we'll address some common questions people have about these issues.

Common Questions

Q: Doesn't the mere idea of the wife being a "*helper*" for the husband indicate that the woman was or is somehow inferior to the man? After all, she's *only* his helper. That doesn't seem right.

A: This question is often raised in objection to the "*helper*" description God has given of the woman. But I believe these types of objections come from a misunderstanding of the words that are used. Being a helper to Adam in *no way* made Eve inferior to him. We've seen that already by noticing that *both* of them were created in the image of God... and there is no greater sign of equal value than that! But beyond that fact, let's consider the word "*helper*" itself.

For someone to be a "*helper,*" it is necessary for the one they are helping to *need* help. In other words, "*helper*" actually points out a limitation or need in the one being helped, not in the one doing the helping. There is no sense in which it should be construed to mean anything derogatory toward the woman. But let's be careful not to fall into an error on the other side. Being the "*helper*" doesn't make her superior either. It simply means she is filling the *role* of a helper.

In addition, if we take the time to notice other ways this word "ezer" (helper) is used in the Old Testament, we will find a remarkable truth! The word is almost always used to refer to the way in which God helps. Some examples...

- Moses names one of his sons "*Eli-**ezer***" and says He did so because "*the God of my Father was my help.*" (Exodus 18:4)
- Jacob, in blessing his son Judah, calls on God to be Judah's "*help*" (***ezer***) (Deuteronomy 33:7).
- Moses also proclaims "*There is none like God, who rides through the heavens to your help* (***ezer***)..." (Exodus 33:26)
- David writes of the Lord, "*Our soul waits for the Lord, He is our help (**ezer**) and shield.*" (Psalm 33:20)
- And on and on and on, throughout the Old Testament (13 other times) the word "***ezer***" is used to describe something that God *Himself* is.
- In fact, besides the description of the woman here in Genesis 2, the only other two times in all the Old Testament that the word "ezer" is *not* used in reference to God – it is used to say that people are *not* the help that God is. (Isaiah 30:5, Ezekiel 12:14).

What is my point ? God uses this specific word (*ezer/helper*) to describe the woman... and He *only* uses it elsewhere to describe Himself! Though our culture may say that the word "*helper*" is a derogatory term, that is simply not true from a biblical standpoint. In fact, quite the opposite is true.

Not only is it used to describe God, but the way God uses the word in reference to the woman, is in a context of blessing and provision, giving to Adam (and all of humanity) a great "help" through the provision of the woman.

Q: So a woman's sole purpose is to help her man? Isn't that a bit limiting and even demeaning to her? She's capable of so much more!

A: Keep in mind, the word "*helper*" is only used to describe her role *in the marriage relationship*. It speaks more of her relationship to her husband than anything else. In fact, that's how God described her.

Think it through... if God has made the man the leader or head in the relationship, with the commission to oversee the direction of the family in the ways of God (as we saw in the last section of lessons), then it makes perfect sense for the wife to be his helper in directing their relationship and their family in those ways too. It is the *way* that they work together in leading their family.

In contexts outside of marriage, there *are* many things a woman is capable of accomplishing! But when those issues arise, there must be great care taken to ensure that biblical priorities are kept in their right order. None of us who are Christians, whether male *or* female, have the liberty to side-step our God-given role to pursue something else. The Bible calls that disobedience, plain and simple. So in the context of a wife who is incredibly talented, she needs to make sure that her first role (helper) is being carried out in a God-honoring way before she fills her life with other things (career, hobbies, etc.).

To put other things first would be like a father who gives food and shelter to neighbor children, but provides none for his own. He's *neglecting* his first and more important role *as* a father to carry out a lesser priority (loving his neighbors)!

I'm not saying that a wife should never work or take on activities outside the home, I'm only saying that she must be careful to ensure that her *primary* role as helper is not suffering because of her added responsibilities those kinds of things will inevitably bring into her life.

Questions for Reflection

- Take some time today to discuss the basic concepts covered so far in this lesson, with your spouse. How do each of you understand it? Are you tracking together or are you responding in different ways?

- Look at your own marriage for a moment. Do the two of you tend to view your relationship as a divinely-designed union, to be lived out for the glory of God?

- What sort of things do you think God is wanting to do through your marriage? How do your individual roles play into that?

- What sort of things do you see that keep people (men or women) from embracing these truths of the wife's role as helper?

DAY 33

<u>A Prayer Suggestion</u>: Start this morning's study by considering this incredible truth: God makes *no* mistakes! One implication of that truth is that whatever God does, He does for a good purpose. Prayerfully consider how that truth relates to the organization and assignment of roles within marriage. Ask God to teach you more about that as you go through today's lesson.

So far we've learned that as a co-bearer of the image of God, Eve possessed complete equality with Adam. Both male and female were fully human, completely loved, incredibly valuable, and given the wonderful responsibility to be God's representatives on the earth. It was from that place of equality that each of them was given a role to play in their marriage relationship.

Adam was to take the lead in moving toward what God had assigned them to do, and Eve was to help him in figuring it out and pulling it off! They were hand-crafted by God to complement each other perfectly. It was truly a match made in Heaven!

We also saw that God first created Adam in isolation, as the only human being. He did so to demonstrate both to Adam and to us, that it was not good for Adam to be alone. That was when God Himself solved that problem by creating Eve as a companion and "*helper*" for Adam. In doing so, He did a very good and needful thing.

He made her to be a blessing, both to Adam and to their relationship together. Without her, Adam was incomplete. With her both of them were complete as God intended.

Without her, Adam was alone. With her, they both enjoyed companionship and intimacy. Without her, God's plans for mankind's rule over the creation could not be fully accomplished, but with her help, they would together be able to accomplish all God had in mind.

It is vitally important that we remember that God's good creation of each original member of the human race was an intentional and specific thing. Adam and Eve were both human and created in the image of God, but were *different expressions* of both humanity and the image of God.

One was male, the other female. Each one, by virtue of their design *as* male and female, contributes in a vital way to what it means to be human, and a bearer of the image of God. As they joyfully lived out their individual, God-given roles, each of them was carrying out the design for which God specifically made them.

In today's lesson and through the rest of the week, we'll begin looking at what it means for a woman to be a helper. As we do so, we will not only build on the truths we've already discovered, but also expand our understanding according to what God's word says about the role and duties of a wife.

Let's begin diving into the scriptures... and as we do, we'll highlight the main instruction given to wives and consider how that instruction relates to her role as a helper. The first scriptural command to wives that we will consider is...

Wives are to submit to their husbands

Colossians 3:18 - *Wives, submit to your husbands, as is fitting in the Lord.*

Ephesians 5:22-33 - *Wives, submit to your husbands as to the Lord. For the husband is the head of the wife as Christ is the head of the church, his body, of which he is the*

Savior. Now as the church submits to Christ, so also wives should submit to their husbands in everything.

1 Peter 3:1 - *Wives, in the same way be submissive to your husbands*

Did you hear it? The can of worms just opened! There is so much dissension, anger, and harsh words spoken over this topic, by both sides of the debate, that it's almost impossible for many of us to get beyond the words to understand the meaning Paul had in mind.

Let's start by looking at the facts. First, there are 3 separate New Testament passages, written by 2 different authors that clearly instruct wives to be submissive to their husbands. It's *not* an obscure idea. It's *not* a gray area or suggestion. It's very clearly stated in words we can understand.

Submission is defined by the role the submitting person plays in a given situation. Citizens submit to their government, students submit to their teachers, employees submit to their employer, children submit to their parents, athletes submit to their coach. And in each of those relationships, it is the *roles* of the people involved that define what the particular submission looks like.

Employees don't submit to their employer in the same way that students submit to their teachers. Neither do citizens submit to their government in the same way that a child submits to their parents. It would be foolish to think that submission in each of these relationships would be identical, because the *roles* and *relationships* involved define the extent of the submission.

In the same way, a wife's submission to her husband has to do entirely with what role he and she play in their marriage relationship. We saw in last week's studies that God has called the husband the "*head*" of the wife. In short, he's been appointed to the role of a Christ-like, self-sacrificing leader in the relationship.

All that means is that he is the one primarily *responsible* before God to take the initiative to see that the relationship and family are moving in the right direction, maintaining health, and growing as God desires... and he is to carry out that role in a way that puts the needs of the marriage and his family before his own.

But there is so much involved in that calling, so much that he could overlook, be oblivious to, or miss – that he cannot do it on his own. So God, in His gracious provision, has given the husband a helper who *is* typically very gifted in many of the areas needed to ensure the family is healthy and strong.

With his wife's willing, intelligent, and competent help the husband is able to be the leader God has called him to be, and she is able to use some of the strongest and most important gifts God has given to her to vitally contribute to their task of creating a godly home and building a godly family.

And here's the most beautiful part of all – as they work together, they develop and display a very strong relational connection between themselves that benefits their entire family, and even the world.

Submission is God's calling of a wife to affirm and honor her husband's role of God-given, sacrificial leadership, and help him in fulfilling God's diverse purposes for their relationship, according to her strengths and gifts.

Submission is not a dirty word. It's the beautiful role a wife plays in working alongside God and her husband to bring their relationship and family into a beautiful image of what God desires it to be.

But that doesn't mean she sits back and passively waits to see what her husband decides to do so that she can dutifully submit to it! Oh no – the role of helper requires a much more proactive and vital input on her part than that! She needs to take initiative in discussing possibilities, directions, and plans for the family *with* her husband. She should feel free to give her input, her insights, and her wisdom to the process of making decisions as a couple.

She should help her husband to see his own limitations, blind-spots, and areas of weakness so that he is able to overcome them. There's an indispensable benefit the entire family receives when the wife *actively* carries out her role as helper to her husband.

A Common Objection

Q: But *Ephesians 5:21* says that all Christians, including husbands and wives are to submit to one another out of reverence for Christ. Doesn't this mean that they are both responsible to submit to each other equally?

A: If the argument that is being made is that since we are to "mutually submit" to one another, then there is no real distinction between what wives are being commanded to do and what husbands are also to do toward their wives – then there are three problems that have to be reckoned with...

First, and most importantly, in the original Greek language, the phrase is not "submit to one another," but rather "submit one to another"- indicating that some will submit to others but not necessarily the other way around. Then Paul gives 3 examples in different contexts (wives, children, slaves) where this kind of "one to another" submission occurs. It appears that his point is not that everyone in the church submits to everyone else in the church, but that those who are in a position where submission is required, should do so out of reverence for Christ.

Secondly, if verse 21 means that there is no

differentiation between the way a wife submits to her husband and the way a husband should "mutually submit" to his wife, then it makes no sense for Paul to go beyond that and say that , wives are to submit to their husbands (*vs. 22*), children are to submit to their parents (*vs. 6:1*), or slaves are to submit to their masters (*vs. 6:5*).

Third, a more obvious problem with appealing to *Ephesians 5:21* in an attempt to avoid the issue is that Ephesians 5 is not the only place this instruction is specifically given to wives. I've already mentioned that there 3 separate New Testament passages, by 2 different New Testament authors, that clearly instruct wives to be submissive to their husbands. And *nowhere* (besides an *incorrec*t understanding of *Ephesians 5:21*) does scripture give the instruction of submission specifically to husbands.

This idea of wifely submission is thoroughly biblical, in a way that is specific to her role as "*helper*" in the relationship. It is part of the way God has created the marriage relationship to work, for His greatest glory. I encourage you to ponder this concept, asking the Holy Spirit to guide you in your understanding. There is beauty here... for your marriage and for the sake of the glory of God. Don't miss it!

In the session we'll spend some time unpacking what submission is not, and what submission is...

Questions for Reflection

- Describe in your own words how men and women are each a unique expression of both humanity and the image of God.

- Honestly, what are your initial reactions to the scripture's instruction for a wife to submit to the leadership of her husband?

- The definition of submission given in this lesson is: *Submission is God's calling of a wife to affirm and honor her husband's role of God-given, sacrificial leadership, and help him in fulfilling God's diverse purposes for their relationship, according to her strengths and gifts.* Write out how you see a wife carrying out each part of the definition...

    - It is God's calling...

    - affirming and honoring her husband's role of God-given, sacrificial leadership

    - helping fulfill God's diverse purposes for their relationship

    - according to her strengths and gifts

DAY 34

A Prayer Suggestion: As you begin today's lesson, ask the Lord to reveal to you any resistance, hesitance, or wrong impressions you may be having about the issue of submission. Ask Him to guide you to what He intends for you to understand.

In her appointed role as a helper, God has given every wife a great opportunity to bring beautiful and tremendous benefit to her marriage and family. One of the ways she carries out this role is through the act of willing, joyful submission to the leadership of the husband God has given to her. But what exactly does that mean?

Does her husband call all the shots while she sits in the shadows waiting for his "*enlightened*" decisions? Or does she "help" him by taking over everything that he seems to be slow about, or incapable of accomplishing? In today's lesson, we'll be considering first, what submission is *not*, and secondly, what submission *is*. We'll begin by looking at an extended passage – 1 Peter 3:1-6.

Wives, in the same way be submissive to your husbands so that, if any of them do not believe the word, they may be won over without words by the behavior of their wives, when they see the purity and reverence of your lives. Your beauty should not come from outward adornment, such as braided hair and the wearing of gold jewelry and fine clothes. Instead, it should be that of your inner self, the unfading beauty of a gentle and quiet spirit, which is of great worth in God's sight. For this is the way the holy women of the past who put their hope in God used to make themselves beautiful. They were submissive to their own husbands, like Sarah, who obeyed Abraham and called him her master (lord). You are her daughters if you do what is right and do not give way to fear.

4 things that submission is NOT...

Agreeing with everything your husband says. - vs. 1

We see this important point in verse one: The woman in Peter's example is a Christian while her husband is not. She has agreed with the gospel message – affirming through her faith that Jesus is the Messiah. But her husband has not done so.

Even though Peter tells her to be submissive to her husband, it is clear that she will not submit to his view of the most important issues in all the world — God, salvation, eternity, etc. So submission *can't* mean that she has to agree with everything her husband thinks.

Even though she is to act in submission toward her husband, she still has her own mind, beliefs, and opinions. Understanding this important point rules out a "Whatever you say, dear..." caricature of a wife's responsibility to submit.

Avoiding attempts at encouraging change in your husband. - vs. 1

The overall point of Peter's instruction is easy to see. He's telling a Christian wife how to "*win*" her husband. This is a wonderful insight into the "*helper*" mission of a woman. She is to be thinking about her husband's well-being from God's perspective. She is to be thinking of ways to help him come to Christ or to become more like Christ. In the end she can't change him, but she can influence him toward godly change.

And as a helper (and at the same time a submissive wife) she *should* be doing so! Some of the most important and powerful ways that my wife has served as my helper is in lovingly pointing out my shortcomings and failures, my sin patterns and pride. In doing so, she helps me to see things that are many times true blind-spots for me.

On another level, her insight into relational issues, social settings, and interaction with people saved me from numerous blunders and mistakes., or has helped me to wisely correct mistakes I've already made. A wise husband will see that his wife can help him in a multitude of ways... and a wise wife *should be* willing to *be* his help.

Putting your husband's will before Christ's will - vs. 1

The Christian wife is a follower of Jesus first and foremost. She cannot, in obedience to the Lord, substitute the will of her husband for the will of Christ. So any situation her husband desires her to enter that is against the revealed will of God, she must say "no" to. Plain and simple, as a follower of Jesus, she cannot follow her husband into actions or choices that are clearly sinful.

Dependence on your husband for spiritual faith or strength. - vs. 1

A good and godly husband should encourage the faith of his wife. But in Peter's illustration, we find a husband who is spiritually checked-out. What's important to notice for our purpose here is that in spite of this husband's lack of interest in spiritual things, the wife is *not* spiritually helpless because of it!

She has her own faith, vibrant and strong, that is dependent on her own relationship with Jesus. She is to develop depth and strength and character in her own spiritual life, entirely because she too has the Spirit of Christ and the Word of God from which to draw. Many times this truth has been turned on its head and wives have been taught that they have to depend on their husbands for spiritual understanding and stability. But in this passage Peter is saying she is not only fully capable of doing so, she is also responsible to do so.

5 things that submission IS...

Built on trust in God – vs. 4-6

Though her husband has been appointed as her "*head,*" a Christian wife does not put her complete trust in her husband. In other words, her husband is not to be the place she looks to for security and strength. She is to put her trust in the promises and character of God.

This is the deep foundation from which appropriate biblical submission flows. Her hope in God extends beyond her husband's ability or trustworthiness, to the point that she has faith that God's design for marriage (including headship & submission) is *right and good*. When a wife puts herself in a place of respectful and intelligent submission, she is putting her trust in God, not her husband. God can handle your husband, you keep your eyes on the Lord.

Fearless – vs. 6

This point is similar to the first, but goes a bit farther. Sarah is held up by Peter as an example of a wife who carried out the right kind of submission toward her husband He says, "*You are her daughters if you do what is right and do not give way to fear.*" Wives who desire to be submissive in a God-honoring way, fight the anxiety that may rise in their hearts as they put their submission into practice.

Think about it for a moment. There are may questions of great concern that wives ask: "Will my husband make a good decision?" "Will he consider *my* desires and needs?" "Is he ever going to lead the family spiritually?"

If she desires to be a wife who submits to her husband's leadership as the scriptures instruct, she will *do what is right* (as Sarah did in her submission) by trusting God in spite of the fears she feels.

An attractive attitude of inner strength– vs. 1-5

Flowing out of the Christ-centered faith of a biblically submissive wife, is a calm, gentle disposition toward her husband. Too often marriage relationships are characterized by harsh criticism, animosity, rivalry, contention, or competition. But the Christian wife understands that she doesn't have to beat him, outshine him, or micromanage her husband. She doesn't have to beat him down, control him, or overbear him so that he does what she thinks is best.

Her trust in God is carried out *through* her submission and is manifested practically in an attitude of strong support, consistent encouragement, and genuine delight in the leadership God has given to her husband – no matter how well he is doing at it!

She seeks to lovingly, carefully, and confidently encourage and support his leadership (or attempts at it). When her strength is used to support him in his areas of weakness (that's being a helper), God does some amazing things.

Given first of all, to Christ – Ephesians 5:22-24

Wives, submit to your husbands as to the Lord. For the husband is the head of the wife as Christ is the head of the church, his body, of which he is the Savior. Now as the church submits to Christ, so also wives should submit to their husbands in everything.

As a wife submits to her husband's God-given role of leadership, she is a living demonstration of obedience to Christ. Notice that Paul says this submission is done "*as to the Lord*."

Should our service to the Lord be done grudgingly, timidly, or fearfully? *No*! It should be done joyfully, with full confidence that what He has called us to do, will be done with the power He provides! So as a Christian wife submits to her husband, she can do so with confidence and joy, knowing that Christ has called her to submission and that He will provide everything she needs to accomplish it.

Respectful – Ephesians 5:33

33 However, each one of you also must love his wife as he loves himself, and the wife must respect her husband.

God is not arbitrary. He gives instruction for a reason. Every command that He gives is meant to meet a need, give protection, and ultimately convey His glory to the world! In this case, He tells husbands that they are to love their wives in the same way they love themselves. Why?

Because their wife *needs* that self-sacrificing love. It is part of the *means* through which the Father provides health, strength, and security to her. He also instructs wives that their submission to their husband's leadership should be carried out in such a way that their husband is respected.

Wives – just as you *need* your husbands self-sacrificial love, He *needs* your respect. It is part of the *means* the Lord will use to help your husband become confident, assertive, and biblically strong in his leadership. Don't hear me saying he deserves your respect, because he may not. But he does *need* it. God has given you as a gift to him, to help meet his need in this area, which will in turn, propel him toward what God desires him to be.

What *is* respect?

- Expressing that he is valuable...
- Encouraging the good you see in him...
- Avoiding cutting or belittling words...
- Leaving the past in the past...
- Believing in him, and in his potential
- Never giving up on what the Lord might do in him...
- Praying for him...

Wives, as you carry out your role of helper, you are taking an active role in building up your marriage relationship and home. God has designed you specifically, specially for that role. You have qualities and characteristics as a woman that make you ideally suited for it.

As you flesh out your role as helper, your husband will receive the encouragement, trust, and affirmation that will enable him to grow more in his role as leader. Don't allow yourself to feel demeaned by the word helper or the idea of submission. Both are beautiful ways in which you are a part of God's plan to bring about His best in yourself, your husband, and in your marriage!

Questions for reflection

- As you read through the section about what submission is *not*, what things did you see that you feel is important for *you* to remember?

- In your own words, describe some of the things that submission *is*. Why are these things important to rightly understand?

- List some of the benefits you see that come to a marriage through a wife accepting and thriving in her role as helper.

- Spend some time talking with your spouse about what submission *is* and *is not*.

DAY 35

A Prayer Suggestion: Ask the Lord to lead you to His heart for marriage as you go through the study today. Ask Him to open your eyes to the important things about the wife's role you've not seen or have been unable to see.

As we wrap up this week's study, there is one more connection we need to make between the husband's role as leader and the wife's role as helper. It's really the greatest purpose for marriage that God has revealed to us – and it is closely tied to the issues of headship and submission. But first let's be aware of two dangers that could side-track our understanding...

- As discussions about headship and submission rage, there's a temptation to pit headship and submission against each other. They do seem like opposites, after all. But the Bible *never* takes that position. God describes each as a blessing that brings health to the marriage when rightly applied. Whenever you hear anyone discussing these terms as if they are opposed to each other, or if you are tempted to think of them that way – remind yourself that God has created them to be perfectly complementary.
- An equal danger is to become so embroiled in those terms and the contentious definitions given from both sides of the argument, that we miss the *real* and *most important* truth behind it all... which is something that very few people seem to be talking about...

Why God created marriage

The most important issue to be kept in mind when we speak of headship and submission is encapsulated in one small word - "Why?" Why did God create marriage in the first place? What is it's purpose? If we can understand the *reason* behind marriage, then we will be able to understand things like submission and headship within the right framework. So, let's take a short journey to Ephesians chapter 5. Paul writes,

> *21 -Submit to one another out of reverence for Christ. 22 Wives, submit to your husbands as to the Lord. 23 For the husband is the head of the wife as Christ is the head of the church, his body, of which he is the Savior. 24 Now as the church submits to Christ, so also wives should submit to their husbands in everything. 25 Husbands, love your wives, just as Christ loved the church and gave himself up for her 26 to make her holy, cleansing her by the washing with water through the word, 27 and to present her to himself as a radiant church, without stain or wrinkle or any other blemish, but holy and blameless. 28 In this same way, husbands ought to love their wives as their own bodies. He who loves his wife loves himself. 29 After all, no one ever hated his own body, but he feeds and cares for it, just as Christ does the church— 30 for we are members of his body. 31 "For this reason a man will leave his father and mother and be united to his wife, and the two will become one flesh." 32 This is a profound mystery — but I am talking about Christ and the church. 33 However, each one of you also must love his wife as he loves himself, and the wife must respect her husband.*

In the early part of my marriage, God used this passage repeatedly to reshape my attitude, understanding, and heart concerning what it meant to be a husband. Over a period of months, as I slowly and prayerfully worked through the passage, the Lord turned on some lights for me that have never gone out! I encourage you to spend some time here on your own, allowing the Holy Spirit to apply its truths to your humble, non-defensive, non-sexist heart.

As you do, be aware of any baggage you might be carrying that comes from our culture and not from the truth of God. Be willing to give up your ideas of what is "fair" or "right" or "emancipated" from our culture's perspective, and seek to understand the substance of what Paul is saying. In doing that, you will come across a glorious truth – the *reason* God created marriage in the first place – and it is found in verse 32...

> *This is a profound mystery – but I am talking about Christ and the church.*

When the New Testament speaks of a "*mystery*" it's referring to something that was previously unknown (at least partially) but *now*, because of Christ, is made clear. From the time of Adam and Eve until the time of Christ, people understood some, but not all of the purposes for marriage. They thought it was for procreation, for completion of each of the partners, for social reasons, etc. But *now that Christ has come*, a fuller meaning has been revealed!

God intends for Christian marriage – the way a Christian husband sacrificially loves his wife and the way a Christian wife respects and submits to her husband's servant-leadership – to *demonstrate* in a flesh and blood way, what Christ's relationship with His church is like! That's the "why" behind the institution of Christian marriage. That understanding puts an entirely new spin on things.

- It's no longer about equality or fairness – it's about being an accurate representation of how the relationship between Christ and the church is supposed to be. Do we or do we not want to accurately represent Jesus' love for His church? Do we or do we not want to be an ongoing, living witness to those around us of the love they can experience through Christ?
- It no longer has anything to do with capability, gender, or rights. It now has to do with a husband or wife's desire to submit to God's plan for showing off His love for the people of earth. We not only get to enjoy the blessings of a God-designed marriage relationship, but we also have the privilege of partnering with God *through* that relationship, to draw others into the family of God!
- Marriage, like so many other things (the rainbow, the Lord's Supper, baptism) is intended to be symbol. But unlike those, marriage is a *living* symbol – a real-life presentation of how Jesus cares for His bride, the church – and how the church is to lovingly and joyfully respond to His leadership.

When we get this idea firmly embedded into our thinking, it makes all the difference in how we think about submission and headship. We can begin to see that God, in His tremendous grace, is allowing us to be a part of reaching those in the world whom He loves. He's allowing Christian couples to live out, as sacrificial as it may be in some cases, a demonstration of that love.

The way I go about loving my wife, sacrificing for her, providing for her, protecting her, can show the lost world how Jesus cares for His own. The way she loves me through her respect, honor, support, and submission to me, shows the lost world how they should respond to the love of Jesus. What an honor that we can be part of such a beautiful symbol! Our healthy, biblical, Christian marriages are one more way the world can be brought to recognize God's love for them!

The Christian calling in general, but also as it relates to marriage, is not about societal or cultural ideas of fairness. The Christian calling is about sacrifice for the sake of others! The Christian calling is about me giving up my rights (like Christ did – check Philippians 2:4-8) and doing *whatever is needed* to hold out the gospel for others to see!

That sort of self-sacrifice is what Christian marriage is supposed to portray! We need to forget about the debate over headship vs submission so that we can *give* our lives so that others can *have* life! Marital roles, as defined in scripture, are part of God's plan to demonstrate that new life to the world!

Questions for Reflection

- In your own words, describe why God created marriage.
- What benefits do you see that a biblical marriage can have on the unbelieving world?
- Explain how headship and submission play into that purpose.
- How do you feel you are doing at demonstrating that kind of marriage? What does your spouse think?
- What practical things can the two of you do to begin making the adjustments needed to demonstrate the love between Christ and His church through your marriage?

SECTION EIGHT

The Principle of Sexual Sanity

DAY 36

A Prayer Suggestion: Ask the Lord to enable you to think of the term "purity" in the way that *He* thinks of it. Ask Him to show you how to adopt this meaning into the application of what you learn today.

In today's study, we'll be returning to Genesis chapter 2 to pick up on some additional ideas communicated there about the marriage relationship. If you recall, God is the one who created marriage, as a relationship specific to one man and one woman (Adam and Eve) and He designed it to function in a healthy, pure way.

When we read that account of God's creation of marriage, we find small statements that are loaded with rich meaning as to what the marriage relationship is to be like. Today we will consider another principle for the marriage relationship, *the Principle of Sexual Sanity*. Let's look at one of those small but powerful statements in Genesis 2:25...

> *And the man and his wife were both naked and were not ashamed.* - **Genesis 2:25**

When God created Adam and Eve and placed them into a marriage relationship, He intended for them to interact and respond to each other in a way that was without shame. Contextually, we are told that they were not ashamed about their physical condition of nakedness!

Sin had not entered the world yet, so there was no reason for them to have any sort of negative connotations about their bodies or their sexuality. They were created naked, and each of them only knew the other *as* being naked, so there was no awkwardness between them because of it.

And, because of the absence of sin in the world, this statement could legitimately be made about the way they related to each other beyond the area of the physical. They were mentally, emotionally, and spiritually "*naked and not ashamed*." They did not experience the barriers and contaminations we do because of sin, so they were quite naturally able to be honest, open, and unashamed with each other on a variety of levels.

That kind of relating may have been pretty natural to them, but for us it's anything *but* natural. Sin has damaged our world, and each of us as individuals. What we have done (sinful behavior), what has been done to us (sinful abuse), and who we are simply by being human (sinners) has limited our ability to be "*naked and unashamed*" with each other.

By pointing out the fact that Adam and Eve were unashamed in the way they related to each other, God is drawing our attention to it... showing us a characteristic of their marriage relationship that is to be true of every marriage relationship. Neither husband nor wife are to be embarrassed, shy, or plagued by guilty feelings when it comes to relating to each other. *That* is why we need to learn *the Principle of Sexual Sanity*!

For the sake of clarity, let's define what we are talking about...

> ***The Principle of Sexual Sanity*:**
> God created marriage to be a relationship of absolute purity between a man and a woman.

This week we'll be unpacking a variety of ways this principle can be applied...

Physical Purity in Marriage

We live in an age and culture where sexuality and nakedness, and anything related to them, are often objects of lewd and distasteful joking. Most every stand-up comedy routine is laced with sexual innuendos or crude jokes. Television shows and movies often include many sexual encounters of various kinds.

Sexuality has become sullied, and is viewed in ways that are far from the purity that God intended. Given these cultural realities, it's no wonder that many couples have no idea how to carry out their physical relationship in a pure way that reflects God's intended design.

Today, we will be looking at some scriptures that show us what the purity of a sexual relationship in marriage should be like.

> ***Hebrews 13:4*** *Let marriage be held in honor among all, and let the marriage bed be undefiled, for God will judge the sexually immoral and adulterous.*

This verse tells us, right of the bat, that Christians are to honor marriage. Of course those who do not have a relationship with Christ are not expected to be true to this scripture. But those of us within the family of God *are* expected to honor and respect the marriage relationship.

This should not be an issue, but sadly it is. Even among Christians, marriage is often joked about in ways that paints it in a negative light. Many followers of Jesus have fallen into the habits of our culture, treating marriage with little seriousness and much cynicism. How is that holding marriage in honor? How is that respecting and delighting in what God has created and called good?

One of the first steps toward sexual sanity is understanding that everything that has to do with marriage – a man, a woman, their differences, their similarities, their covenant with each other and God, their love, their sexual relationship, their children – all of these things are to be *honored* by Christians. That means they are to be held in high regard.

This is especially true between marriage partners. A husband and wife need to learn to love their marriage. No more jokes about marriage being a "ball and chain." No more jokes about it being a "life sentence." Marriage is to be honored by all believers.

In addition, disciples of Jesus are to honor and love each other in a way that does not disparage or make fun of the differences that make the two of them unique. Marriage is intended to be between a man and woman – each made intentionally and uniquely different by God *in order* to make marriage what He intends it to be! So jokes about men and women in general are out of place in the Christian marriage.

Next, the writer of Hebrews tells us that the marriage bed, a euphemism for the sexual relationship within marriage, is to be "*undefiled*." That is a word we don't use much in our day and age, so we should be careful to make sure we know what it means. The dictionary defines the word this way:

> ***undefiled*** **–** *adjective* – 1. free from stain or blemish.
> 2. not having its purity or excellence debased.

So the sexual relationship between a married man and woman is to be free from stain or blemish. There is to be no hint of wrong or impurity in the way it is carried out. From the context we can tell that the writer is speaking of sexually immoral things, such as adultery, that are to have no place in marriage.

This would include the use of pornography by married couples (which is nothing more than watching adultery or immorality for the sake of sexual arousal), or engaging in sexual activity either together or separately that includes additional partners. Sexuality in marriage is intended to be exclusive, pure, and private.

In addition, the sexual relationship is not be a thing to be joked about or exposed to the eyes or ears of others. Jokes or inferences made to others about the sexual things that happen between a married couple are inappropriate. To joke in this manner is to open the door to your bedroom and let others get a glimpse, however slight, of what goes on there. That debases the purity and excellence of the sexual relationship that God has created to be enjoyed in purity and holiness.

The sexual relationship that God has provided to you will be a greater joy as you protect and defend it against the impure and destructive ideas and actions that threaten to sully its purity.

Questions for Reflection

- When you think of the attitudes our culture has about sexuality in general, how would you describe them?

- How do you think these attitudes make God feel?

- Do you think that you have adopted any of these attitudes? If so, in what ways?

- Can you think of bad habits or wrong thinking that you have fallen into regarding the sexual nature of your marriage relationship? Discuss this issue with your spouse?

- Are there any changes you need to make together?

DAY 37

<u>*A Prayer Suggestion*</u>*:* Thank the Lord for what you have learned so far in this course. Ask Him to enable you to retain and apply the things that He is continuing to show you.

Today we will be turning to the New Testament, to further explore what the Scriptures have to say about the sexual area of your marriage. More specifically we'll be looking at some principles the Lord gives that will benefit you greatly if you will put them into practice consistently.

> ***1 Corinthians 7:1-5*** *Now concerning the matters about which you wrote: "It is good for a man not to have sexual relations with a woman." But because of the temptation to sexual immorality, each man should have his own wife and each woman her own husband. The husband should give to his wife her conjugal rights, and likewise the wife to her husband. For the wife does not have authority over her own body, but the husband does. Likewise the husband does not have authority over his own body, but the wife does. Do not deprive one another, except perhaps by agreement for a limited time, that you may devote yourselves to prayer; but then come together again, so that Satan may not tempt you because of your lack of self-control.*

The people in the church at Corinth had written to the Apostle Paul, asking him a variety of questions about how to live out the truths of the Christian life. From this paragraph we can see that they had asked him something about men, women, and sexuality.

His answer to them gives us some very important understanding of how husband and wife are to view the sexual area of their relationship. Today we'll look at the first part of what Paul says to them...

Avoiding Sexual Immorality – vs. 2

God has provided marriage as the "safe haven" in which sexual activity is to be enjoyed. Indulging in *any* kind of sexual behavior outside of marriage is considered "*sexual immorality*." Throughout the course of a marriage relationship husband and wife will both be tempted to engage in sexual behaviors that are immoral in nature, things that are not within the bounds of their relationship together.

Here we are taught that a sexual relationship between husband and wife, enjoyed regularly, will help to satisfy the very natural sexual desires each of them have, so that the pull of temptation is not so strong. This has very important practical implications.

- Each marriage partner should make sure that they are caring for the other sexually, so that they do not experience unnecessary sexual temptation.
- In order to do this, open communication about each partner's sexual needs, desires, and cycles is vital information to know! How can you meet a need if you don't know exactly what it is?
- The sexual component of your marriage is more than a physical act. When healthily pursued, it can be a safe-guard for your relationship.

- Your sexual availability to your spouse is a loving act of ministry to them, enabling them to maintain personal purity and devotion to you and to the Lord.

Sexual Ownership – vs. 4

Notice what the passage says... " *For the wife does not have authority over her own body, but the husband does. Likewise the husband does not have authority over his own body, but the wife does."* Becoming one in marriage means that each of you has certain "rights" or "privileges" in regard to the body of your partner. Practically this means...

- *Both* marriage partners have the same "right" in regard to the other. Neither of you should ever "trump" the other. You should come to decisions about the sexual component of your relationship *together.*
- There is to be no awkwardness between you in relation to the sexual aspects of your relationship. Each of you needs to be free to love the other physically and to be loved by them physically. If you don't feel that is true of your relationship already, you can grow in that area through honest, clear communication. It will be difficult to discuss sexual matters at first, but the more you do, the easier it will become, and the healthier your sexual relationship will be!
- But the "*authority*" you have over your spouse's body is *never* to be used in a way that is inconsiderate of them as a person. If your understanding of this principle is leading you to think that you have a biblical right to force your spouse into sexual actions or situations that he/she is not comfortable with, then you are misunderstanding the spirit of this passage. In all things, love for your partner must prevail!

Questions for Reflection

- Given what today's scripture says about the sexual relationship in marriage, how do you feel *you* are doing at helping your partner avoid unnecessary temptation?

- Are you able to see your part in your sexual relationship as a ministry of love to your spouse? If not, what makes it difficult?

- On a scale of 1 to 10 (1 = terrible, 10 = excellent) how do you feel that you and your spouse are doing at communicating honestly about sexual matters?

DAY 38

A Prayer Suggestion: Spend some time in quiet before the Lord. Try to be aware of the reality that He is present with you at this very moment. Let your confidence in His desire to teach and help you grow as you do. Ask Him to reveal helpful truths to you today.

Today we will continue examining what the New Testament says about the sexual aspects of your marriage relationship. Picking up where we left off in the last lesson, we will be returning to 1 Corinthians 7:1-5...

> ***1 Corinthians 7:1-5*** *Now concerning the matters about which you wrote: "It is good for a man not to have sexual relations with a woman." But because of the temptation to sexual immorality, each man should have his own wife and each woman her own husband. The husband should give to his wife her conjugal rights, and likewise the wife to her husband. For the wife does not have authority over her own body, but the husband does. Likewise the husband does not have authority over his own body, but the wife does. Do not deprive one another, except perhaps by agreement for a limited time, that you may devote yourselves to prayer; but then come together again, so that Satan may not tempt you because of your lack of self-control.*

Regular not sporadic – vs. 3-5

- Notice we are told that neither partner should "*deprive*" the other of sexual relations under normal circumstances. Regularity is important.
- The regularity of your sexual relationship is to take priority. You have to be intentional to provide time together and to protect it. The stresses and pressures of everyday life can easily crowd out your times of intimacy.
- In order to get into a habit of regular intimacy together, you may have to discuss how your schedules and responsibilities impact your time and energy levels... and schedule your times together with that in mind. It's not uncommon for well-meaning couples to be worn out at the end of a long day and not be "up" to sexual interaction.
- Though it may seem awkward or artificial at first, don't shy away from setting "appointments" on your personal calendars for this aspect of your relationship. You make appointments for other things that are less important, why not make sure this vital part of your relationship is not inadvertently neglected?

Sex is *not* a weapon – vs. 5

- It's not uncommon for couples to use sex as a weapon. When a disagreement arises one might use the sexual relationship to manipulate the other to a place of forced agreement. But this is absolutely *wrong* to do!
- The sexual relationship was created by God to bring you closer together. It is a physical expression of the growing unity between you, not something to be used as a weapon.
- An attitude that uses sexual interaction in the manipulative ways is worlds away from the healthy,

loving, others-centered attitude married individuals are expected to be growing in toward their spouse.

- Using sex as a tool of manipulation against your spouse damages your relationship instead of helping it. Should that kind of behavior happen between you, the two of you will begin to see each other as adversaries and opponents, not partners.

Abstain only by agreement – vs. 5

- The situation depicted is one where the two of you sense a great need for God's guidance in your relationship or a situation you face. In such circumstances, you may decide *together* to abstain from sexual intercourse, like a sort of fast, so that both of you can utilize that time and energy to focus on prayer about the issue at hand.
- Don't miss the importance of such things being done only *by agreement*. It can be very hurtful to your spouse if you decide on your own to abstain from sexual relations... even if it is for a very good reason. Make sure that you talk about your intentions and thoughts regarding sexual fasting so that you have the opportunity to come to agreement.
- With this idea of regularity in mind, consider how times of required separation from each other (business trips, etc.) figure in. Should you make sure that you meet each others needs right before the trip? Immediately upon returning?
- The only exception to this principle is in the case when job-related situations require long periods of separation. In such times much prayer and regular communication can help to carry you through in a faithful way.

Don't forget your enemy – vs. 5

- All it takes is a look through the newspaper or a quick glance at the television to see how prevalent sexuality is in our culture. Satan knows the power of hormones, emotions, and physical actions that are a part of sexuality... and he's ready to exploit it every chance he gets. Be on guard against His schemes (Ephesians 6:11).

It is clear that God, as the Creator of sexuality, has a great deal to say about the way in which it is carried out. He's got great ideals in mind for what sexuality can do in and for a marriage relationship that is centered around Him. While that is true, it doesn't mean that there aren't problems to be addressed. Our next session will begin addressing some of the sources of contamination to the purity of your marriage relationship.

Questions for Reflection

- Do you feel that your sexual interaction with your spouse is regular enough? Set aside time together to talk about that question. How close is your opinion about this question to that of your spouse?

- As honestly as you know how, evaluate whether there have been times when you have used your sexual availability as a weapon against your spouse. If so, do you understand the damaging, ungodly impact that has on your relationship?

- If you see such practices in your past or present, spend some time before the Lord in repentance. Make sure to confess and repent to your spouse also.

- Brainstorm for a moment: In what ways can you better improve the regularity of your sexual relationship? Scheduling it on your day planner? Setting aside a regular time or two each week? Taking on a different attitude about your sexual relationship? What comes to mind?

- Talk with your spouse about how he/she sees your sexual relationship being vulnerable to Satan's attacks. Make a plan together for how you will combat or prevent such attacks.

DAY 39

<u>A Prayer Suggestion</u>: Today's session may be a bit difficult for you, because it has to do with your sexual past. Ask the Lord to enable you to recall what is needed to help you move toward a healthier place in regard to your mindset and actions regarding sex. Ask Him to sustain you through the painful memories that may arise.

In many ways sex is the icing on the cake of your relationship together... and as such God desires it to be enjoyable and fulfilling. But the sad truth is that the power of sin in our world, and more specifically in our lives, has damaged many of us in regards to sexuality.

Today's lesson, though potentially painful, will take into consideration how your past sexual experiences and understanding might be serving to corrupt and contaminate your sexual relationship with your spouse.

Sources of Contamination

The past, and in particular the experiences we've had in the past, can be very powerful things. They have served to shape our thoughts, attitudes, and in many ways our behaviors. When those past experiences were positive, we have gleaned benefit for our present and future lives.

But when those experiences have been painful, sinful, or untrue, then we have most likely become victimized by those things to some degree. What God intends for our sexual relationship as marriage partners can be contaminated by those things from the past.

Let's take a few moments to consider some possible source of contamination...

Ungodly images or ideas about sex

Statistics show that the average age at which most people who have seen pornography are first exposed to it, is 11 years of age. What that means is that most everyone reading this has at least seen pornography at some point in the past. If not pornography, most have seen movies or television shows with explicit sexual content. So? What's the big deal?

The issue is that those types of depictions of sex show a very skewed idea of what it is all about. If you've picked up wrong ideas about sex, they may have wedged themselves into your mind, and you could be believing that the portrayals you've seen are what sex should be like. But it's not.

Sexuality, like everything else, takes time and work to happen in a healthy way. It requires a great deal of communication, understanding, and patience – unlike the one-night-stand scenarios so frequently depicted in popular media. A wrong understanding here can lead to...

Wrong expectations

When your husband or wife doesn't do it the way you've seen it done, you may begin to question things. "What is wrong with me?" "What is wrong with him/her?" "Why aren't our experiences as 'sizzling' as that?"

The reality is that though there are aspects of the sexual relationship that are quite natural, there is a good deal of it that has to be learned over time and specific to your spouse. You can't expect your sexual relationship to be like any other, especially those you've seen in the media.

Feelings of shame or embarrassment

Depending on how you were raised and what you were taught about sex, you may feel like it's "dirty" or "wrong." But sexuality within marriage is in no way dirty or wrong. God made sex to be a blessing and joy to married couples.

Attitudes and feelings of this nature short-circuit your ability to enter in to times of meaningful sexual intimacy with your spouse. You need to be convinced of the truth – that sex in marriage is a joyful and wonderful thing about which there is no need to feel shame or embarrassment.

A performance mentality

Again, the media has had a huge impact on most of us in this area. You may have the idea that every sexual encounter with your spouse should be full of passion, deep emotion, and that you should be like that woman or man on the TV.

The reality is that sexual interaction in marriage is not about performance! There should be no other expectation except that you and your spouse are going to express your love for each other as best you know how.

Feelings of inferiority or fear of rejection

Sex is not an isolated action or event. It is connected to the other parts of your life, both past and present. If the circumstances of your life have caused you to develop insecurities or feelings or worthlessness, it is possible that they will have a detrimental impact on your sexual relationship. Both partners should do their best to affirm, build up, and encourage the other both during and outside of the sexual relationship to counteract such past hurts.

Lack of commitment to the marriage relationship.

If either partner senses that the other is not fully "in" the relationship, then he/she may be hesitant about all things sexual. Dedicated attention by both spouses to *the Marriage First Principle*, *the Cleaving Principle*, and *the Unity Principle* will go a very long way toward providing peace of mind for both of you in regard to the level of commitment each of you has to your marriage.

Insensitivity to your partner's sexual needs.

It's not uncommon for one partner or the other to become so enthralled with the sex act that he/she forgets to pay attention to the other's sexual needs.

Make sure that your sexual relationship is a "two-way street." Sometimes that might not always mean that sex takes place. Some people enjoy cuddling, closeness, and warm words just as much or more than they do the act of sex. That means that once again, open communication is needed so that both of you can know what the other receives as a loving act. Learn to talk openly and act on what you learn.

Past abuses – sexual or otherwise.

When one or both partners have experienced abuse in the past, the difficulty and pain of entering into a healthy sexual relationship can be excruciating. The similarities between what happened during the times of abuse and what takes place in a married sexual relationship are so similar that it's next to impossible to separate the two, mentally.

While very difficult to overcome past abuse, it is not impossible to do so... and with the Lord's help, great healing and recovery can occur *through* your relationship.

Some helpful tips...

- Patience. Don't expect things to change quickly. Trust God's timing.
- Love never fails... and there are great and powerful aspects of emotional and spiritual healing that come from the Lord as you learn to express genuine and unconditional love. If your spouse has experienced sexual abuse, your understanding and deep concern will go a long way in helping them to heal over time.
- Tenderness and care. Go slow and take it easy. When you truly love your emotionally wounded spouse, you will be more concerned about their security and growth than you will be your own sexual needs. *Care* for them, don't just tolerate their hurts. Healing can come as you faithfully show the love of Christ!

Past sexual relationships.

1 Corinthians 6:15-16 *Do you not know that your bodies are members of Christ? Shall I then take the members of Christ and make them members of a prostitute? Never! Or do you not know that he who is joined to a prostitute becomes one body with her? For, as it is written, "The two will become one flesh."*

- Notice what we are told here: *"he who is joined to a prostitute becomes one body with her..."*
- While the passage is speaking specifically to the issue of sexual interaction with a prostitute, the principle it teaches is true for any sexual relationship.
- When you engage in sexual activity with a person (any person) there is a type of unity that occurs between you.

- That unity is not broken simply because the relationship ends.
- As a result, many people enter into a marriage relationship with multiple connections of this kind tagging along behind.
- On a spiritual level, those connections, created through sexual interaction, need to be broken.
- As a believer in Jesus, you have the authority in Christ to repent of, renounce, and shed those connections.
- And you should! Do what you need to do in order to break those connections and truly make oneness with your spouse possible!

These are just *some* of the possible sources of contamination to the purity of your sexual relationship. Regardless of the details of your situation, the Lord Jesus can and will help you overcome them as you do your part in seeking His help and working toward a healthier marriage.

Begin with honesty, before God and with your spouse. Talk about your sexual past together, with a view toward repentance. Then go to the Lord together, with repentant and trusting hearts, asking Him to navigate the waters ahead and lead you to a healthier sexual relationship together.

Questions for Reflection

- Take some time to carefully consider the listed contaminations to a healthy sexual relationship in your marriage. List the ones from *your* background that you think could be contributing to problems in your relationship.

- Write down some of the potential contaminants from the past of *your spouse* of which you are aware. Begin praying for your spouse in regard to these things. Ask the Lord to begin the process of healing.

- Set aside time to discuss the areas each of you see that may be contaminating your sexual relationship. Remember that each of you will need patience, tenderness, and love to be expressed about these things. In discussing these things, get the help of a mature believer if you need it.

DAY 40

A Prayer Suggestion: Thank the Lord for His faithfulness. Thank the Lord for marriage. Thank the Lord for *your* marriage, and the plans He has for it. Thank Him for His desire to make your marriage strong and healthy. Ask Him to open your eyes more fully to the bright future He has in store for the two of you.

The goal of this week's topic has been to open the door to some of the complicated and difficult issues that have to do with sexuality in your marriage. In doing so, you've hopefully become aware of some areas that could use some attention. And perhaps, you've received some encouragement about how sufficient the hand of God can be in your marriage when you each approach such things with an open and willing heart.

In today's final lesson on this topic, we're going to state some of the plain, but vital guidelines that you need to plant deep in the soil of your soul. They need to become a part of you, so that you will be vigilant in defending and nurturing your relationship and the sexual aspects of it.

Overriding principles

1. Each partner has an obligation to pursue sexual purity with their spouse and to safeguard the marriage against any threat to it.
   - Do whatever it takes to put yourself in a place to maintain purity with your eyes. Learn to have eyes only for your spouse.

- Find ways to regularly talk to each other about the sexual aspect of your marriage. As times change, so will your needs and desires – and you need to stay up to date on what each of you needs and desires.

2. Make sure that *you* are not causing fear, inhibition, or self-protectiveness in your spouse. Your relationship should be one of love, acceptance, patience, and care.

3. Remember that your sexual availability to your spouse is a ministry of love to him or her. Don't allow personal preference or busy-ness to get in the way of this valid way that you can love him/her.

4. Do your best, together, to set standards for your home that do not allow outside influences to bring any kind of impurity into your relationship.
   - Re-evaluate your television, movie, and magazine choices.
   - Protect your Internet access with filtering software or accountability software.
   - Do what you need to do in order to make your home a safe haven from impurity.

5. Be constantly on guard – Satan is relentless in his desire to derail your marriage.
   - Become habitual in your prayers against his influence and attacks.
   - Draw close to the Lord so that you will have the discernment and wisdom needed to notice when Satan is attempting to subvert your sexual relationship or marriage.
   - Pray for your spouse, to be protected from Satan's attacks in the sexual area.

Questions for Reflection

- Can you imagine your sexual relationship with your spouse being a thing of joy, purity, and delight? If so, why? If not, why not?

- Do you regularly pray for your spouse in this sexual area? If so, how could you do so more regularly or effectively? If not, make a plan to begin.

- Set aside a time together to specifically pray, as a couple, for God's best in your sexual relationship. Express your heart's desire for how you want to love your spouse, and how you want the entire interaction to honor the Lord.

SECTION NINE

9

What Next?

My prayer is that the last 40 days of study have been helpful and encouraging to you and your marriage. As our Creator, the Lord has been so gracious to reveal Himself and His will for us regarding life and marriage. I trust you have seen Him and His will for your marriage in these pages.

My encouragement to you is to continue what you've learned in these pages in the days to come. Keep communicating, keep applying what you've learned. Keep working out these principles in the daily life of your relationship together. With God's help, you will continue to grow as a couple, and bring greater and greater glory to Him as you do.

Should you hit some snags along the way, don't get discouraged. Difficulty is part of what the Lord uses to bring us to maturity (Romans 5:3-5, James 1:2-4), and we are unwise to seek to avoid it. Let the Lord use those times to further craft your souls and your marriage into a better image of His relationship with His church.

Finally, get help if you need it. There are many healthy Christian couples who are much further down the marriage-road than you are. Seek them out. Watch what they do. Ask them questions. Spend time alongside them. The Lord will use the example of others to help you along your way.

May God richly bless your marriage, so that you will point others to Him accurately and joyfully!

Carey Green
September 26, 2011

Why Free Resources?

The Gospel message was given freely by God, and I believe it should stay that way... even as far as to include training materials for those who are spreading and upholding the gospel. I want to make it easy for churches and people, those with huge budgets as well as meager, to be able to adequately train those the Lord has entrusted to them.

To that end, I'm providing downloadable resources free of charge and hard copy resources at prices that cover the cost of printing and time required to produce the resources. I have no desire to "get rich" from the resources I produce, only to help the church ***be*** the church.

You can find all of my free resources at
http://thepfjournal.wordpress.com

If you would like to make a donation to support me as I endeavor to carry out this ministry, it is greatly appreciated. You can do so in two ways:

Regular Mail
Carey Green
c/o Community Church
P.O. Box 242
Leadville, CO 80461

Internet:
Paypal © to
faithforward@gmail.com

May God bless your work for His name's sake!

Carey Green

About the Author

Carey Green has been blessed to be in Christian ministry since 1988 when he began his first youth internship while attending Colorado Christian University. During those years he has served the church in a variety of areas including youth ministry, worship, administration, small group coordination, associate pastor, and lead or senior pastor.

He has been married since 1989 to his best friend and ministry partner Mindi, and has 5 children.

With over 20 years of ministry experience, Carey is available to consult or speak on a variety of topics, including church conflict, candidate search process and interviewing, Elder training and assessment, men's ministry, family & marriage ministry, parenting, and church health - as well as biblical preaching.

You can find many down-loadable free resources Carey has created at his blog: http://thepfjournal.wordpress.org